A Woman's Voice

Dec. '01

For Mary Kaye—

In appreciation for
your dedicated service &
caring ways.

Warmly,
Marcella

A Woman's Voice

Biblical Women: Divine Wisdom Transformed into Action for Today's Woman

Marcella Bakur Weiner and Blema Feinstein

Jason Aronson Inc.
Northvale, New Jersey
Jerusalem

This book was set in 11 pt. Hiroshige by Alpha Graphics of Pittsfield, NH, and printed and bound by Book-Mart Press, Inc. of North Bergen, NJ.

Copyright © 2001 by Marcella Bakur Weiner and Blema Feinstein

10 9 8 7 6 5 4 3 2 1

Library of Congress Cataloguing-in-Publication Data

Weiner, Marcella Bakur.
   A woman's voice: biblical women-divine wisdom transformed into action for today's woman / Marcella Weiner, Blema Feinstein.
      p. cm.
   Includes bibliographical references and index.
   ISBN 0–7657–6149–1
   1. Women in the Bible—Meditations.   2. Bible. O.T.—Biography.
   3. Jewish women—United States—Conduct of life—Anecdotes.
   I. Feinstein, Blema.   II. Title.
   BS575.W395   2000
   221.9'22'082—dc21   00–038970

Printed in the United States of America. Jason Aronson Inc. offers books and cassettes. For information and catalog write to Jason Aronson Inc., 230 Livingston Street, Northvale, NJ 07647-1726, or visit our website: http://www.aronson.com

To the memory of my sister, Lillian *a"h*, whose courage and purity of love are rooted in our hearts forever.

Marcella Bakur Weiner

To the memory and merit of my husband, Alvin *a"h*, who dared to give me the support needed by a woman who must share her love of writing with her love of a very dear husband. And with deep gratitude to our two daughters whose love and understanding have melted barriers greater than I could ever handle alone.

Blema Feinstein

Acknowledgments

Our deepest thanks to Arthur Kurzweil, our editor, and his assistant, Diane Jehle, for their caring work on behalf of this book. We extend our appreciation to Ruth Mayerhoff for her technical support and to Carla Hanauer of West Side Judaica in New York City for her patience in selecting books of relevance to the writing of this one. We wish to extend our heartfelt love and appreciation to Will, Marcella's husband, and to Alvin a"h, Blema's husband, for their sensitive feedback to the creation of this manuscript. In addition, we offer our profound appreciation to our clients, students, and mentors, from whom we have learned so much; Rabbi and Rebbetzin Chaim Bausk, Rabbi and Rebbetzin Jonathan Feldman, Rabbi Meir Fund, Rabbi Aryeh Kaplan z"l, Rabbi Yitzchok Kirzner z"l, Rebbetzin Frumi Kirzner, Rabbi and Rebbetzin Yehuda Kelemer, Rabbi Shmuel Lipszyc, Rabbi and Rebbetzin Tuvia Teldon, Rabbi and Rebbetzin Moshe Weinberger, Rebbetzin Tziporah Heller, Rebbetzin Leah Kohn, and Mrs. Esther Wein.

And for their personal interest and nurturing, we thank Richard and Carol Bobbe, Heidi Elson, Ethel Galowitz, David and Naomi Greenberg, Ephraim and Shifra Gross, Lois Grossman, Tina Kahn, Valerie Kruger, Tamara Laufer, Miriam Lourenzo, Joyce Mechanic, Murray and Tziporah Roter, Sheila Schloss, Rita Schwalb, Dr. and Mrs. Yehudah Sorscher, Deanna Springer, Batsheva Teitlebaum, and Ellyn Weinstein.

Table of Contents

Introduction

A Woman's Voice
Introduction

When we, Marcella Bakur Weiner, Ph.D. and Blema Feinstein, Ph.D. came together to write this book, we were seeking a connection, subtly but deftly hidden in the stories of Judaism, between women then and women now. In the voices and actions of our ancient ancestors, we discovered powerful hints that inspire the lives of women of all ages in our time. Women, single or married, can benefit from stories retold and reinterpreted through the lens of our own eyes.

The basic information is carefully culled from traditional Jewish sources: The Babylonian Talmud, Midrash, Rashi, Ramban, Or HaChayim, The Chasam Sofer, and many others, as well as from men and women scholars of our time: Rabbi Yitzchok Kirzner zt"l, Rabbi Moshe Weinberger, Rebbetzin Tziporah Heller, and Rebbetzin Leah Kohn. Stories you will find here come also from our own experiences working with, for Blema her students, and for Marcella her clients in psychotherapy. We were constantly intrigued by how their stories and lives interface meaningfully with the stories of women, some of whom lived thousands of years ago. From Sarah, women can learn when and how to say, "No." From Rebecca, who struggled to bring heaven and earth together for her descendants, today's woman can find inspiration as she seeks to turn away from "models" in our society who concentrate on materialistic values alone, and look instead for a balance between spirit and body toward a richer and meaningful life. Leah, "The Unwanted Wife," a leading force in the saga of Jewish history, provides a powerful incentive for women who do not feel cherished and yet learn to create love and beauty in their lives and that of others. Rachel, the essential feminine woman, kind, self-sacrificing, extraordinarily compassionate, puts aside her own jealousy to do what is right, accomplishing what the greatest men could not do. A strong support for today's woman, Rachel inspires compassion for others that overrides our own human frailties. We have chosen twenty-one different stories to illustrate the struggles, suffering, and ultimate triumphs of a wide selection of extraordinary women. The inspiration they offer is ageless. It is our hope that in reading this book, you will arrive at your own answers, making conscious personal connections with fascinating women of our past. The cross-fertilization of ideas and lives makes this book unique. Dedicated to the sanctity of human life, we believe that our spiritual tradition looms greater than ever, that Judaism holds a universal and timely meaning for women of today and of tomorrow.[1]

---

1. In a brilliant lecture, Rabbi Moshe Weinberger has set forth a concept of two covenants made by God with the Jewish people. One is well-known and essentially intended for men. The second covenant addresses the women. When we are in trouble, in the darkness of various kinds of exile, just sustaining ourselves may require consistent effort, nurturing, taking care of the mundane that keeps us going. In such times the power and the love to work through anything we are in comes from the woman. Rabbi Weinberger's tape, "A Mother's Tears (Chayeh Sarah/Chanukah)" Congregation Aish Kodesh (718) 868-8331.

I

Beginnings

⟪ 1 ⟫

Sarah: The Woman
Who Could say "No"

The most powerful corrective given to man is woman!
Unfortunately, Eve, the first woman to be created, used her
talents to persuade her husband, Adam, to transgress when she
encouraged him to eat of the tree of knowledge of good and evil.
Happily, that first error was turned around several generations later
by another woman named Sarah.[1]

God directed Abraham to listen to the voice of his wife, "(in) all
that Sarah saith unto thee, hearken unto her voice; for in Isaac shall
seed be called to thee."[2]

---

1. Genesis, *The Pentateuch and Rashi's Commentary*, trans. Rabbi
Abraham Ben Isaiah and Rabbi Benjamin Sharfman (Brooklyn, NY: S. S.
& R. Publishing Company, 1949), 23:2. Unless otherwise indicated, all
biblical quotations are taken from this edition. "*Baba Bathra*," *Nezikin* 2,
The Babylonian Talmud, trans. Maurice Simon (London: The Soncino
Press, 1978), p. 233. Dr. Blema Feinstein, "Between Holy and Profane,
The Torah View of Separation," *Bas Ayin* (January, 1995), pp. 21ff.

2. Genesis, *The Pentateuch*, 21:12. "*Megillah*," *Mo'ed* 4, *The
Babylonian Talmud*, trans. Maurice Simon (London: The Soncino Press,
1978), p.82.

"She [Sarah] foresaw [the future] by holy inspiration; hence it is written 'In all that Sarah hath said unto thee, hearken to her voice.'"
"*Sanhedrin*," *Nezikin* 3, *The Babylonian Talmud*, trans. H. Friedman, (London: The Soncino Press, 1978), pp. 471–472.

MALE AND FEMALE—DIFFERENCES

The male, to reach his potential in spiritual growth, is challenged by obstacles he has to overcome. His maleness, passion, physical strength, strong ego, eagerness to be heroic, thrusting power, push for independence, and single-mindedness are his natural inheritance. Yet passions, ego, and overdriven self-reliance are easily misdirected and may become barriers to his spiritual development. To help him overcome or minimize such barriers and allow his full spiritual energies to spiral, a man must study, pray at particular times each day, wear special garments when praying to help him enter into a more private relationship with God. Patience and the willingness to surrender and seek emotional help when needed often require the encouragement of a woman.

Different from man, woman is like the angelic figures who, in our literature, seem to appear as needed and then recede from view. Endowed at birth with potentials for spirituality for which her male counterpart must continuously struggle, she can be his silent support.[3]

SARAH—KIND AND GENTLE,
STRONG AND COURAGEOUS

Sarah is one such woman. Both kind and gentle, she is also strong and courageous. When her child, Isaac, is born, she becomes a wet nurse for other mothers less fortunate than she. Along with her generous husband, Sarah keeps the tent open to all in need of food, drink, shelter, and rest. Her deep concern for the nation that would descend from her is obvious at the time of her death. Crying for her

---

"Her husband was crowned through her, but she was not crowned through her husband." Genesis, *Midrash Rabbah*, I, trans. Rabbi H. Freedman (London: The Soncino Press, 1983), p. 455.

3. Rebbetzin Tzipporah Heller is an ongoing source of information and inspiration on women in the Torah. Secular studies include C. Gilligan, *In a Different Voice, Psychological Theory and Women's Development* (Cambridge: Harvard University, 1982); Judith V. Jordan and others, *Women's Growth in Connection* (Wellesley, MA: Wellesley College Stone Center, 1991).

people who would be martyred in the future, her tears ascend to Heaven, her final plea: "Please help my children." Inspired by the models of her husband and her son involved in the near sacrifice of Isaac, she understands that martyrs through the ages will be strengthened in the dedication to God.[4]

Nevertheless, Sarah's greatest legacy for women may be her ability to distinguish between positive and negative energies in her home and, even at the risk of appearing harsh or cruel, to say "No" to the negative.

Unlike Sarah, Abraham was prepared to accept the negative behavior of his firstborn son, Ishmael, and the insolence of Hagar, the mother of Ishmael. Raised in the home of Terach, who created idols for an idol-worshipping society, Abraham was able to rise above his first family and become the founder of a new nation. He believed that like himself, Isaac could become a stronger person raised in a home where he had to overcome the negative influence of his half brother, Ishmael.[5]

But Sarah, created according to the will of God, understood that children must be raised in a home pure of all negative influences. The mockery perpetuated by Ishmael distressed her. She knew that joined with mockery is the tendency toward lust and idol-worship. We who mock whatever is sacred place ourselves above the Creator as if to say: "This is ridiculous. I alone know what makes sense."

---

4. Genesis, *The Pentateuch*, 17:16. On Sarah's qualities, see Rabbi M. Miller, *Sabbath Shiurim 5729*, third ed. (Gateshead, England: Gateshead Foundation for Torah, 1982), p. 35.

Genesis, *The Pentateuch*, 23:2; Traditional interpretation holds that Sarah died of grief, thinking that Isaac had been sacrificed: "Genesis," *Midrash Rabbah* II, third ed., trans. Rabbi H. Freedman (London: The Soncino Press, 1983), p. 511, We learn another view from Rabbi Yitzchok Kirzner z"l in a shiur given on November 12, 1987: Sarah, who could access all her potentials when in exile, is our foremost female model: her concerns embraced not only her immediate family but also generations of Jewish descendants to come. She died crying to God to help the Jewish people who, inspired by her saintly husband and son, would die as martyrs.

5. *Chasam Sofer, Commentary on the Torah, Bereshis*, adapted by Rabbi Yosef Stern (Brooklyn, NY: Mesorah Publications,1996), p. 104.

Placing ourselves at the center of the universe, we focus on appeasing our sexual appetites, and we worship possessions that feed the ego. Parallel to this is a pulsing eagerness to destroy whatever is worthwhile in life.[6]

HAGAR: ADORED DISCIPLE

Prior to Ishmael's birth, Sarah thought of his mother, Hagar, as an adored disciple and servant. And so she was. Because Sarah remained barren, she urged Abraham to marry Hagar as a second wife and have a child who Sarah would raise as her own. But this was not to be. Pained and disappointed, Sarah watched Hagar's coarseness and arrogance intensify and widen to include others in her negative thoughts about Sarah. Most women subjected thus would become depressed and withdrawn, retreating from life and avoiding confrontation, but Sarah stood tall.[7]

Her hopes for Hagar shattered, Sarah knew that rejection was absolutely necessary. She understood with her entire being that her son, Isaac, and not Ishmael, the son of Hagar, was the one who must inherit the Jewish teachings of Abraham and Sarah. Sarah's natural ability for understanding the need for boundaries gave her the courage to act with clarity and firmness to cleanse her home of negative influences. To Abraham, she says: "Cast out this bondwoman and her son; for he shall not be heir, the son of this bondwoman, with my son, (even) with Isaac."[8]

A woman of the tent, self-contained and free to exercise toughness when needed, Sarah meets each moment head-on.

SARAH IN PHARAOH'S HAREM

Earlier in the story, because of a famine in Israel, Abraham and Sarah go down to Egypt. There, Sarah is taken into the harem of the Pharaoh. Unlike her tent adorned by the light of Sabbath candles

---

6. Genesis, *The Pentateuch*, 21:19; Rashi note 9, pp. 96–97.

7. Genesis, *The Pentateuch* , 16:1–6.

8. Genesis, *The Pentateuch*, 21:10.

that burned from Sabbath to Sabbath, protected by clouds of glory and the holiness of the woman at its center, the harem of the richest king in the world holds no meaning at all for Sarah. When God, in all His wisdom, sent a punishing angel to smite the Pharaoh with an affliction so that he could not touch Sarah at all, this kind and gentle woman called out, "Smite him, smite him!" Because she is true to her deepest self, the beautiful and cultured pleasures of the palace could do nothing to alter the reality of who she was: wife of Abraham, mother of Israel, and servant of God.[9]

EVE AND SARAH: TWO WOMEN
AT POLAR EXTREMES

Looking at Eve, the first woman, and Sarah, mother of Israel, we see two women at polar extremes. Where Eve could not sustain boundaries, Sarah created them. Eve was given specific instructions that she and Adam could eat of the fruit of the trees of the Garden but not of the tree of the knowledge of good and evil. But beguiled by the serpent, an alien intruder, and crossing boundaries, Eve is persuaded to disobey the commandment of God and persuade her husband to sin as well. Ejected from the Garden thousands of years ago, humankind still reverberates to this one act. Failure to maintain boundaries, we remain in exile.

While an entire people may live in exile, so too do individuals who separate from their true selves. Conversely, the story of Sarah portrays a woman committed to boundaries and the moral responsibility this entails. Sarah asks Abraham to send Hagar and her son Ishmael away. She knew how to say "No" to what was undesirable.

THE ABILITY TO SAY "NO"

The ability to say "No" is the foundation of conscious choice. While we say about children aged two that they are in the throes of the

---

9. Genesis: 12:10–20, *The Chumash*, The Stone Edition, general editors Rabbi Nosson Sherman, Rabbi Meir Zlotowitz (Brooklyn, NY: Mesorah Publications, 1993), notes pp. 57–59. "Leviticus," *Midrash Rabbah* IV, third ed; trans. Judah J. Slotki (London: The Soncino Press, 1983), p. 413.

"terrible twos" with their constant repetition of this powerful two-letter word, it is a healthy part of development.

Entering the world unable to differentiate self from mother, the theme at the beginning is "I am you and you are me." We all know the horror stories of children who are not cared for, and the disastrous effects that abuse and neglect in their early years have on them throughout life. Dramatic studies show that babies as young as six months of age, when left without a caregiver to hold them, and touch them frequently while making cooing sounds, developed depression similar to those in adults. Some died. When caregivers were assigned to them, the miracle of reversibility occurred. The babies bounced back into life. No pill. No special technique or gadget. Merely someone who was there for them, a person physically and emotionally giving, allowing the necessary merger that "I-you-are-the-same" to be made. For the infant, having been part of the mother for a full two-thirds of a year before birth, needs to be weaned into separation once born. Like putting a baby on solid food, it is a slow and steady process until the young child learns to be truly a separate person. At two when they say "No," they are affirming that individuation. "I am not you and I don't want to do what you want me to do" is the loudly acclaimed message.

That is if all is going well in the household. If not, when parents are unavailable both emotionally and physically, demanding that the child conform to their wishes or needing the child to live out the unfulfilled dreams and wishes of the parent, the ability to say "No" becomes submerged. "If I say 'No', " thinks the child, "I will lose whatever it is I have. I can't afford that. So I will conform, hold back and not say what I truly feel, want, and need."

Just as we eject a food that we feel is harmful to us, "No" is cast out of the system.

WOMEN'S INABILITY TO SAY "NO"

Women in particular are subject to this inability to say "No." We are more apt to wish, above all, to please another person. Nurturing caregivers, we may, unlike Sarah, diffuse or lose our own voice.

The following is not an uncommon modern-day story: Helen is known in her community as a caring, loving woman. Recently, a friend some years younger was feeling sad; she had lost her job and was having "a tough time of it all." Empathic, Helen invited Jean to come and stay with her. Helen was a housewife by choice, in a good marriage with a man to whom she felt very close. They had four children, ranging in age from three to fourteen. Helen was a busy woman. Jean came to visit and all went well for a time. Everyone seemed to get along. Helen went out of her way to please her friend, make her feel wanted, the children engaging her as did Henry, the husband. A few weeks went by, but Jean did not talk about leaving. Instead, she began to take Helen for granted and, like Hagar, she treated Helen in a disparaging way. "Can't food ever be served on time in this house?" she would ask impatiently. Or "Helen, I think your figure is really ruined, what with your having four children and all." When one of the children would watch television or play a game during the afternoon, Jean would shout at them to be quiet for she was "resting and needed some peace." Helen wanted to ask her to leave but delayed and delayed. "Will that not make me a mean person?" she thought, or "Is it not my duty to take care of those who need me?" And so Jean stayed with Helen who became more and more depressed until, finally, she became ill. "Everything wrong seemed to be happening to my body," she said. When we do not listen to our core self, the inner voice, the voice of our soul, illness may result.

Nothing comes upon us suddenly. There are signals, signposts along the way. When we ignore the signs, sent to us by God to keep us on our unique path, we plunge into a state of chaos. Called depression, acute anxiety, panic, fear, nonfunctioning, we suffer. What can we do? How can we sensitize ourselves to the cues?

Listen to our hearts, feel our body's rhythms, our breaths as they change. Our body sends us warnings. Heed them. And then, take action. Do something! Move the stagnant energy called pain and suffering out. Breathe freedom in. Act. Helen, like Sarah, finally did just that.

After a time of acute suffering, Helen told Jean to leave. After this, spiritually stronger than ever, Helen bounced back. The household returned to its balanced, happier state.

WOMEN, THE NATURAL NURTURERS

Throughout history, women have been the natural nurturers, the healers. From the beginning, they developed skills and talents that led to survival: cooking, basketry, agriculture, even home building. Learning about plants for food and medicine ensured survival of the species, and woman became the primary caregiver. Then and now we care for one another: in labor, in childhood, and in old age.

In their glorious life-affirming roles, women generously give love energy to others. A God-given quality, it is intrinsically precious. Yet, with it, women must honor boundaries. In the case of Helen and Jean, the violation is obvious. Similar to Hagar and Sarah, Jean shows disrespect and ingratitude to Helen. At times, however, disrespect is more subtle but equally insidious, especially in relationships we have with those closest to us. The spouse may show disrespect. Not overtly abusive, it is, nonetheless, a serious lack of honoring the other that can cause a drop in self-worth.

MARTIN AND SHEILA, A COUPLE IN CONFLICT

Martin and Sheila had been married for twelve years. A perfectionist himself, Martin is constantly making Sheila "feel stupid." He does not say this directly. "It would be easier if he did," says Sheila. "Then I could nab him right then and there. But his subtlety hurts even more." Self-denigrating, she adds, "Maybe I really am stupid after all." He finds fault with whatever she does. "Why are you doing it this way?" he asks. She may reply with a scathing, sarcastic glance. But her husband has humiliated her. Deeply embarrassed, she retreats into herself, becoming sad and aloof. Reacting, Martin assaults her even more, calling her "moody, unreachable, overly sensitive, a mental case." Martin is mocking Sheila, a put-down that pierces her heart. Contrary to God's intention when he created woman as a "helpmate," one who would provide appropriate support or challenge when called for, Martin's behavior obliterates her role and turns her, instead, into the type of person who, with so little sense of self, has lost her ability to make choices.

Humiliating or shaming another person is a form of murder. Where murder may be justified, for example, in self-defense, insults never are. They strip us of our likeness to God. They create distance between us and our Creator.

WOMEN AS AGENTS OF CHANGE

What can Sheila do to change this? First, she must acknowledge to herself that Martin is violating her sense of being, her very personhood. She must feel, not dismiss, her pain.

Responsible unto herself, Sheila needs to become self-caring, reestablishing her connection to God. Action in both words and deeds must follow. Martin needs to be informed of his behavior. Choosing words carefully so as not to inflict pain on another, Sheila is selective in her communications. Not with psychologizing or endless, nonfruitful analytic dialogue that is resented by the other, but, instead, by short, incisive, direct statements, similar to our eminent forebearer, Sarah. Sheila can say to Martin, "You cannot speak to me this way. You are crossing the boundaries of respect, and I will not tolerate this." With clarity and directness, she needs to ask for some change in him. In asking what he is going to do to make the necessary changes, she can offer to help. Thus, as soon as she hears him return to his habitual track of disrespect, she can stop him, assisting him to catch himself in time. Since he has an acute, if critical, eye, she can suggest that before attacking her, he think through what he wishes to say or write it out. A spiritual life means that we think before we speak, ask ourselves, "How will these words affect the other person?" And crucially, "Will they serve humanity?"

Martin, giving thought to what he says, will be encouraged to consciously act on his feelings rather than be an immediate reactor. Step-by-step, Sheila can guide him to the point where he becomes less offensive. With her assistance, he can learn to monitor himself. Concretely, like a true guide, she can say, "Martin, up to this point, you are fine and I appreciate what you are saying. But here, you have crossed over into insult. Can you stop yourself before that? It would be most helpful to our marriage." Newly aware of this, he would slow down to permit himself to become an observer of his behavior, the core of maturity.

If motivated by his love for his wife and respect for himself, though habits are hard to change, Martin will make the effort. If not, Sheila may need to speak to a respected person, a member of the clergy, a professional counselor, a close friend or relative who is competent to take on that role. Or she may seek out and join a women's support group. Her boundaries of self must be protected.

GENDER DIFFERENCES

Current studies of the human brain seem to indicate that gender differences are innate.[10] Researchers discovered what many have already observed. When children ages 2 ½ –8 were given an array of toys, boys favored sports cars, fire trucks, and Lincoln Logs. Girls played with dolls and kitchen toys, often "playing house." The article stressed that differences continue throughout the lifespan. For example, men suffer heart disease at a younger age than women. In general, women have a more moderate response to stress.

Women lead more with heart than head. Psychological tests report that men and women see the world differently.[11] Where men are best at rotating three-dimensional objects in their head, women are best at reading emotions. They have a gift of being able to understand the feelings of others in a most sensitive way. Even when words are garbled, women have a sense of what is being said. The researchers suggest that women were given this skill so that they could interpret the speech of toddlers before they can fully express themselves.

CHOOSING BOUNDARIES, CHOOSING LIFE

Despite the dramatic changes in our contemporary society, women continue to deal with life's challenges as they have since the beginning of society: as nurturers, caregivers, protectors of the home; with clear vision and courage to act, we emulate Sarah. Whether housewife and mother working in the home or outside the home, she is the "in charge" person. Nothing runs smoothly unless she is there, taking care of home-related events. Like Sarah she needs to

---

10. Christine Gorman, "Sizing up the Sexes," *Time* (January 20, 1992), p. 42.

11. —— p. 44.

be aware of all negative influences. Sensitive to any evidence of impurity or danger, she can keep the home pure. Crossing of boundaries is not to be tolerated.

Choosing to respect our boundaries, as did Sarah, we choose life.

Let Sarah be our guide!

⊸ 2 ⊱

Rebecca: A Balanced Life

BACK TO AN UGLY AND ESSENTIAL SOURCE

Abraham and Sarah are the first Jewish people in the wold, an identity well earned, sought after, and embraced by Abraham, a very wise man who used his mind to decipher the meaning of the world, the meaning of life for humankind. Sarah is the prophetess who looks deep into the future of her descendants and understands with her entire being what it is that God wants. Clearly, without grandchildren there will be no future. With no son there will be no grandchildren, and without a very special type of wife, there will be no children at all. We have seen in our first chapter how significant a role Sarah played in the life of Isaac, her son destined to bring in the future. We focus now on her daughter-in-law, Rebecca. To find a suitable mate for his son, Abraham sends his highly trustworthy and dedicated servant, Eliezer, back to Ur of the Chaldees, to the ugly but essential source where Abraham, Sarah, and all the matriarchs, the mothers in Israel, are born.[1]

---

1. Genesis, *The Pentateuch and Rashi's Commentary*, trans. Rabbi Abraham Ben Isaiah and Rabbi Benjamin Sharfman (Brooklyn, NY: S. S. & R. Publishing Company, 1949), 24:2ff. Genesis II, *Midrash Rabbah* II, third ed; trans. Rabbi H. Freedman (London: The Soncino Press, 1983), pp. 521–539.

Of the many excellent traits necessary for the daughter-in-law
of Abraham and Sarah, the central one is *chesed*, kindness to all
life, a love of giving for the sake of giving, and a joy in giving that
embraces the fortunate ones who are open to receive.[2]

ISAAC'S TRAIT, JUSTICE, REQUIRES
A WIFE OF KINDNESS

Isaac's trait of justice called for an *ezer kinegdo*, a helpmate whose
kindness would balance her husband's sternness. How ironical that
this kindest of women emerges from a horrendous background in
which she had to stand alone, no models, no companions, not one
person to help her. Her only model was her older brother, Laban,
well-known to us as a thief par excellence, who will later try to
decimate his holy son-in-law, Jacob, and steal his grandchildren
from the path of God to follow his idol-worshipping and stealthy
way of life in which only the glow of gold matters. The father of
Rebecca, Bethuel, is so evil that God removes him from the scene
before he can obstruct the marriage of Rebecca to Isaac.[3]

The "models" given to Rebecca are subject to greed, envy, and
lust. Nevertheless she becomes a model for us, as one who knows
how to use a tarnished background as a reminder of the kind of
people she vehemently distrusts, people she will never emulate and
never befriend. One would think that, faced later with Esau, a son
who manifests all that she has come to reject, Rebecca would throw
up her hands in helplessness, perhaps dejection. Instead she takes
a mighty step in the right direction and, aided by God, assures the
future of Jacob and thus of the Jewish nation.

---

2. Genesis, *The Pentateuch*, 24:67; Rashi notes p. 233. Genesis II,
Midrash Rabbah II, pp. 538–539. Rebbetzin Tziporah Heller, "Created in
His Image," *Hamodia*, November 6, 1998, p. 43.

3. Genesis, *The Pentateuch* , 25:20; Rashi notes p. 239. Rebbetzin
Heller: "Coming from her family, Rebecca knew who she did not want ever
to be," notes on lecture, "Women in the Bible: Creating Your Own Support System."

OUT OF HER DARK PAST

Out of her dark past, Rebecca sifts what is of value in earthly matter to strengthen the spiritual qualities here. The harmony and balancing of which we speak is the merging of earth and heaven: in concrete terms, the balance of body and spirit in which the body serves the spirit, and health and money can be used to further the work of the soul. Life is treasured; Rebecca, at great self sacrifice, saves the life of the son who must carry on the tradition of Abraham and Sarah, teaching him to value the physical as well as the spiritual and so ensure the future of the Jewish people.[4]

TWO BASIC LIFE FORCES:
PHYSICAL AND SPIRITUAL

We will not here detail the events of the lives of Isaac and Rebecca, but focus rather on their two sons. In a large context, Esau and Jacob represent two basic life forces: physicality and spirituality. Esau loved to hunt, to conquer, to control. His passion was bottomless; his physicality swallowed all that could have been spiritual. Had he chosen to follow the Jewish path, he could have provided a powerful model of spiritualized passion, complementing the pure spirituality of his brother Jacob.[5]

Because Esau would not take on the role of servant to God, his mother understood that Jacob would need to represent the worldly as well as the spiritual, physical earthiness as well as rarefied heavenliness. However, there was no way that Jacob would easily accept the balanced role posed by his mother. His resistance was strong. He argued with Rebecca: this was dishonest, it was thievery; Esau and his holy father would curse him. Gentle Rebecca stood strong

---

4. "Rivka [Rebecca] . . . wanted the material blessings to go to Yaakov [Jacob]." Rabbi Ezriel Tauber, "You Can Take It With You," *Jewish Observer* (February, 1995), p.13. "His material possessions are more precious to the *tzaddik* than his own body because their acquisition required more effort." Rabbi Zev Leff, "Shabbos, part 23," *YATED NE'EMAN* (July 23, 1999), p. 53.

5. Genesis, *The Pentateuch*, 25:27–34. Rashi notes p. 244–247.

and clear. With the help of an angel, we are told, they carried Jacob bodily toward the great father's room. Once inside, Jacob stretched his soul. Overcoming his inborn reticence, he speaks, "I am Esau, thy firstborn, I have done, according as thou badest me. Arise, I pray thee, sit and eat of my venison, that thy soul may bless me."[6]

The worldly blessing prepared by Isaac for Esau is now given to Jacob. Later, Jacob will receive the spiritual blessing as well, for it was always intended for him. Isaac knew well that Jacob was born to holiness. What Isaac had not known, that Jacob had to take on the worldly stance as well, was now shown him thanks to the maneuvering of his wife.

Once Esau learns of his loss, the life of Jacob is in danger. At great sacrifice, Rebecca sees to it that her beloved son escapes, never to see his mother again. She suggests to her husband that it is time to send Jacob north to find a wife, and so Isaac sends Jacob "to the house of Bethuel thy mother's father."[7]

Jacob's journey is not an easy one, but in time, thanks to his wives, he slowly takes on the worldly role foreseen as essential by his mother.

Perhaps more than any other single trait, the balancing of soul and body remains a challenge for all of us. We speak of it in terms of sanctifying the mundane, spiritualizing the body, elevating the lowly. Regardless of the terms used, we can look back to Rebecca and, like her, come to acknowledge the importance of the physical in making possible the work of the spiritual.

THE SUCCESS OF A JEWISH MOTHER

Was Rebecca successful in fulfilling her mission to instill a worldly presence in a son whose initial thrust was totally spiritual? It is not to say that Jacob had a smooth and easy life on earth; not at all. He suffered from a brother who wanted to kill him, from a conniving father-in-law who sought to destroy him, the twenty-two-year loss of his favorite son, Joseph, who was destined to unify the family,

6. Genesis, *The Pentateuch*, 27:1–41.
7. Genesis, *The Pentateuch*, 28:2.

the kidnapping and rape of Dina, his only daughter: "Few and evil have been the days of my life."[8]

Jacob did not embrace the physical at once; his progress was slow. On the way to find his wives, he had a dream that has become famous: the dream of the ladder above which God stood calling on Jacob to begin to climb upward. We are told that Jacob refused to climb the ladder because of his deep-seated fear that should he climb, his descendants would be successful in worldly goods. Unlike his mother, Jacob still believed that spiritual growth could not join with worldly success.[9]

TO TREASURE OUR POSSESSIONS

Many years later, a father of ten sons and one daughter, Jacob learned otherwise. Coming to meet his murderous brother Esau, Jacob planned several strategies to avoid being destroyed. The night before all this would happen, he remembered that he had left several jars of oil on the other side of the river. He went back alone to retrieve these possessions.

Some say that this was wrong, even foolish, to risk his life in the dark just for a few jars of oil. Others say that this was a turning point in the awareness of Jacob. At last he understood that his possessions were gifts from God that had to be treasured, properly cared for, and used.

That night Jacob encountered the angel of Esau and was not overwhelmed. What did the angel want to accomplish? Surely the angel could have overcome Jacob in a second were that his purpose. No! All the angel wanted was to take Jacob away from the strong connection he had with God, with the spiritual dimension.[10]

This was a struggle for dominance: if Esau won, spirituality was lost; if Jacob won, spirituality won. But it was a standoff! Physical

---

8. Genesis, *The Pentateuch*, 47:9.

9. Genesis, *The Pentateuch*, 28:12–17. "The concept that one can serve *Hashem* [God] even from the material perspective is entirely Jewish." Rabbi A. Leib Scheinbaum, "Peninim Ahl HaTorah . . . " *YATED NE'EMAN* (September 11, 1998), p. 103.

10. Genesis, *The Pentateuch*, 32:25–33.

and spiritual belong together. The spiritual is stronger because it connects with the Source, but without the physical component, spirituality goes nowhere on earth. Not overcome, Jacob is then told that, added to his name, he is to have a new name: "Israel" (favored of God).[11]

As Israel, this son of Rebecca becomes father to twelve sons who head the twelve tribes from which the Jewish nation is molded. He represents the *midah* (character trait) of *emmes*, of truth. Forever etched into our spiritual genes are his blending of *chesed* and *gevurah*, kindness and sternness, the resolution of qualities expressed by Abraham and Isaac and made possible by Rebecca.

To outwit the enemy, Jacob had to draw on a certain kind of trickery in his relationship to Esau and to Laban as well. Initially, he had to deceive his father into believing that the worldly blessing was going to Esau. Since we are not on the level of the spiritual giants of our history, we are taught not to emulate such behavior. However, there are resources within us that may be hidden or repressed, resources that God wants us to draw on when faced with challenges sent from above. We learn from the stories of Rebecca and her son, Jacob, how to reach for the higher level within which to move toward a harmony of physical and spiritual.

HUMANKIND STRUGGLES BETWEEN PERFECTION AND DEFICIENCY

While creation in general consists of two basic parts, the physical and the spiritual, humankind consists of two opposites, a physical body and a spiritual soul. Nothing else in all creation shares this quality.[12] The physical centers around us experience through our senses: sight, hearing, touch, taste, and smell. The spiritual comes to us through our transcendental soul. Different from each other, the physical and spiritual are nevertheless bound together. Created for the purpose of coming close to God, humankind juggles between

---

11. Genesis, *The Pentateuch*, 32:29.

12. Moshe Chaim Luzzatto, *The Way of God*, fourth rev. ed., trans. Aryeh Kaplan (Jerusalem and New York: Feldheim, 1983), p. 77.

deficiency and perfection. Inherent in this is the ability to reach for perfection, accomplished through free will, the making of conscious choices. Created with both a Good Urge (*Yetzer Tov*) and an Evil Urge (*Yetzer HaRa*) we have the power to move in whichever direction we choose. When we incline toward the physical, we move in the path of the material; the soul, in contradistinction, leans toward the spiritual. A necessary state of tension exists continuously between the two. But if the soul is in ascendancy, it elevates not only itself in its push toward perfection but the body as well. If the physical outpaces the soul, the soul is lowered and the person moves further away from nearness to God. Where the soul is primary, the physical body can be purified so that it too derives pleasure from the spiritual.

Our state in this earth world of ours consists of two things: our own intrinsic nature and the environment of home and society. Immersed as we are in the physical and material aspects of this world, we can reach toward perfection through our activities on earth. With the blessing of free will we can transform darkness into light.[13] However, this transformation is not an easy journey. Caught in the frenetic materialism of our contemporary society, we may become ensnared by it, and despite good intentions, become captive to its seductions. Laurel did. And then made the correction.

LAUREL'S DISAPPOINTMENT
IN HER LOT IN LIFE

One of three children and the only girl, Laurel and her parents, Sam and Frieda, lived in an upscale neighborhood several notches above what they could afford. They acquired the apartment when Sam offered the landlord his skills at taking care of this and an adjacent building. A small, comfortable if modest, residence, it gave Sam easy access to his store where he sold a variety of household goods. They were devoted parents; the only unbridled tension was that of money: the lack of it. Laurel recalls Frieda's lament when holidays were in the offing: "Sam, I'm not a magician. The dollar is not a rubberband.

---

13. ——— p. 65.

I can't stretch it." Mild-mannered and seldom angry, Sam would smile and placate his wife: "Frieda, darling, I'm doing what I can. Wait and see. Things will get better. We have to trust." A dedicated man, his prayers and mealtime blessings would become ever more passionate. Frieda would join him, but Laurel sensed her mother's sadness and disappointment in her lot in life. These nagging feelings persisted. Somehow, there were the "have's" and the "have nots," she and her family in the latter group. She saw it all around her: in the ease with which others spent money in her father's store, the pride the women and their children took in their dress, their offhand way of spending money. She felt deprived. Though never openly expressed by herself or her parents and brothers, there was a feeling that nonentitlement to the material comforts of this world was their destiny.

Budding into womanhood, Laurel's good-looks attracted attention. With long, dark curly hair, large, expressive hazel eyes and pert, even features, she was "a beauty." A match was easy to find.

When she and Carl met and sat in a hotel lobby sipping tea and getting to know each other, they concluded that they had found their soul mates. Life after marriage did a turnabout. Coming from an affluent family, Carl was both pious and successful in business as well. Monies poured in and Carl, an attentive husband, lavished much on his wife. After a year, a son was born and two years later, a daughter. Closets were bursting, the house was luxuriously furnished, holiday and Sabbath tables displayed a gourmet assortment of the best. Laurel was heady with the newness of this lifestyle. Much time spent on shopping, she was forever seeking and accumulating. Good-natured, Carl would ask, with a laugh, "Laurel, how many days in the week are there to wear all of this?" or "Look at all these shoes. Are you growing more feet?" Still he was generous and proud of his wife's taste and good-looks. On every special occasion and in between, he showed his joy in buying her jewelry. It became a special game. Producing a small box, he would casually say, "Laurel, my love, I bought you another *chatchka*. It's nothing. But I thought it would sit well on your eleventh finger." After placing the ring, he would lift her hand, and with feigned gallantry kiss each finger.

THE BUBBLE HELD A LETHAL CRACK

Life was a bubble. Her son and daughter were growing up to be people of good character, outstanding students, and caring and attached to their parents. But the bubble held a lethal crack: Laurel's obsession with the material. A demonic pull within her screamed, "I need, I want, I must have," plunging her deeper and deeper into a horrifying abyss. Though dimly aware, she could not stop. Even during prayers, concentrating as best as she could, asking God to deliver her from the fury within, she felt possessed. Laurel was becoming a slave to earthly passions, the spiritual silently shrinking. And then it happened.

LAUREL HAD A DREAM

The house was quiet and all were asleep. The children were in their beds and my husband, Carl, and I were also sleeping. Suddenly, almost as though it were truly happening, I smelled smoke. I thought, at first, that it was just an illusion but a minute later realized it was real. I could sense there was a fire somewhere. I was frantic to escape. But how? What? I thought of my jewels. I had to save them. I ran to my jewel box, putting on rings upon rings, bracelets upon bracelets, necklace atop necklace. The smoke was getting thicker and thicker. I was choking. I ran toward the door leading out. Then I stopped in horror. I heard a shriek jab into the air: "Oh, my God, my God, what am I doing?" I had left my children and husband behind. And I started to shake, feeling the bed pulsating beneath me. Then I woke, feeling the tears wet on my cheeks. I lay there, quietly staring into the darkness, horrified but in gratitude that it was only a dream.

Laurel, sensitive and perceptive, knew that is was "more than just a dream." A wake-up call, it was sent to alert her to the path her life was taking and, crucially, to the need to change. Our dreams, at times divinely inspired, can give us directions as clear as signposts on any road. But we have to read them and take heed.

Laurel was appalled that her instinctive push toward saving herself was to grab her jewels. This revelation shocked her to the core; she recognized that it paralleled the life she was living. As with other such revelations, the shock propelled her toward the truth. But this was just the beginning. Knowledge must now be transformed into action.

LAUREL MADE A TURN

Reeling from the impact of her awakening, Laurel made a turn. Understanding that her obsessive attachment to things was out of step with spiritual alignment, she would have to take dramatic action, making the revelation concrete. Addictive behavior is no easy thing to cast aside. Determined, she called her rabbi to ask if she could donate some of her clothing to the needy. He told her to pack some boxes and bring them to the synagogue. If she had other items, she could include them, for new immigrants had joined the Jewish community. She acted quickly. Going through her closets and all the rooms in her home, she put aside a stack of clothes and other items as well. Recognizing that she should not be obsessive or addictive in the opposite direction, she would not get rid of everything. She gave her full mind, body, and spirit to the task, fully enjoying it, knowing that she was now sharing with others. She asked the rabbi if she could help in some volunteer status; he connected her with several nursing homes in the area. She became one of the most beloved of volunteers, helping feed older women who, due to arthritis or other debilitating ailments, could not feed themselves. She thought, "I am using my physical self to do this mitzvah. My hand, a part of my physical self, is the server in this task." Since she dressed neatly and stylishly when she appeared at the nursing home, some of the women began to groom themselves or ask an aide to help them. Formerly unkempt, hair was now combed, a dress properly fitted and, most of all, as they waited for Laurel to come and see them, a look of radiance shone on their faces. From time to time, she brought gifts: a handwoven handkerchief, a scarf, a sweater, and, for those able to read, a book. She brought photos of herself and her family and asked the residents to show her their family albums. Both staff and residents called her an angel. She formed deep and lasting connections in her work and thought of going back to school to learn a profession wherein she could help others.

Carl was proud of her. He revealed that for some years now, he had felt that he was losing her love. She seemed, he said, to be there, but unavailable to him for a deeper connection. Believing that he was losing her, he tried to compensate with gifts. As in many such families, he unwittingly become a co-conspirator. Laurel said, "I never suspected that he was feeling so alienated, so desperate. But now that I am back, he says I am once again his beautiful queen, his precious *malka*."

Laurel's sense of balance was established. She knew in her heart that the physical must serve the spiritual. Neither is to be ignored. Placing the physical in proper alignment with the spiritual, she was creating the necessary harmony between the two. Like Laurel, we too can bridge the distance between heaven and earth. In this, we elevate all of humanity.

‹❨ 3 ❩›

Leah: The Unwanted Wife

" . . . Rachel was of beautiful form and beautiful appearance. And Jacob loved Rachel."[1]

Rachel was the younger sister, and her father tricked Jacob into marrying Leah, the older and less beautiful sister. In response to Jacob's angry and resentful demand for an explanation, Rachel's father Laban replies: "It is not so done in our place, to give the younger before the firstborn." Laban will give Rachel to Jacob as the second wife. Eventually Jacob will acquire four wives from whom the twelve tribes of Judea descend.[2]

THE GENTLENESS OF RACHEL

Had all gone well according to the desire of God, Jacob would have married Rachel at once. Esau would have married Leah, and the Jewish nation would have descended, six tribes from each marriage, modeled after the gentleness of one family and the passions of the other. The gentleness and quiet courage of Rachel, sufficient for Jacob, would have been a source of peace to soothe the sharpness of truth unsheathed.

---

1. Genesis, *The Pentateuch and Rashi's Commentary*, trans. Rabbi Abraham Ben Isaiah and Rabbi Benjamin Sharfman (Brooklyn, NY: S. S. & R. Publishing Company, 1949), 29:17–18

2. Genesis, *The Pentateuch*, 29:26.

Laban thought that he alone was foiling the plans of God. Lacking all-seeing knowledge of God, he did not realize that the marriage of Leah to Esau would have to be foregone. Ordained in Heaven that Leah would marry Esau did not mean that she would have nothing to say about that marriage. What is suggested is that the bond between Leah and Esau was a very strong one; "made in Heaven" reveals a power beyond any earthly connection. Bound thus to Esau, Leah cries year after year, knowing that tears, strong enough to cause permanent damage to her eyes, will weaken the heavenly bond as well.[3]

JACOB: SPIRITUAL AND WORLDLY

That Laban tricked Jacob is not the entire picture, for Leah joined her father in deceiving Jacob to marry her. Surely she understood that this would create a serious strain on her relationship with her husband, that she might well remain the unloved wife, and that Jacob might sunder their marriage. What then did Leah hope to achieve? We are told that the morning after the trickery, Jacob confronted his new wife: How could she have done such a terrible thing, placing herself before her younger sister who was so beloved of Jacob that he had been willing to work for seven difficult years, putting up with the thievery of Laban, just so that he could marry Rachel? Leah's reply is fraught with meaning. She reminds Jacob that he had tricked his father, Isaac, in order to be given the worldly blessing intended for Esau. Did that not, she asks, mean that Jacob had to have the woman intended for Esau? Jacob had taken over the mission intended for Esau, a worldly role; thus, in addition to Jacob's spiritual destiny, he now had to develop a worldly involvement as well. Leah had been selected by heavenly forces to become the *ezer kinegdo* (help meet) of the passionate and earthbound Esau, to affirm his behavior when it reflected God's will and to correct and redirect him when he stepped on negative ground. Now that Jacob

---

3. Rebbetzin Leah Kohn, The Matriarches: Rachel and Leah, The Tears of Jewish Mothers," tape lecture (November 20, 1996), drawn from Tanchuma and interpreted by Shem Mishmuel (Yeshiva Sochatshov 1974), p. 34.

had entered the domain of the earthly, does he not require an *ezer kinegdo*—a Leah—suited to redirect him in his new role?[4]

We do not find Jacob readily responding to Leah's wisdom. Just as it takes many years before he can absorb his mother's advice that he take on the blessing intended for Esau, just so does it take him many years to absorb Leah's wisdom. Not until Leah has borne four sons, Rueven, Simon, Levi, and Judah, does Jacob come to understand and accept God's will that, along with Rachel, Leah must be a mother in Israel. At long last, the deepest desire of Leah to be accepted as a mother in Israel is realized.[5]

Perseverance, in the midst of storm and the buffeting of harsh winds that test our endurance, our faith, our courage, even our clarity of thought, means we can hold to what is good and right. Sealed in that perseverance are two other traits of character modeled by Leah: a deep well of gratitude from which Leah draws the ability to give a name to her fourth son: Judah (Yehudah) is cognate to Hebrew words that mean praise, thanksgiving, gratitude. The term "Yehudeem" (Jews) comes from Leah's choice of a name for the son whose birth brought forth in Jacob an understanding of the magnificence of his first wife.[6]

LEAH: GRATITUDE AND THANKSGIVING

With gratitude and thanksgiving, we inherit from Leah the potential to acknowledge our dependence on a power in the universe that is kind to those who may be misunderstood, as was Leah and others in our own time.

A third quality may be the most difficult of all to develop: Women generally have a great need of validation. Sociologically and psychologically, there may be substantial reasons for our need

---

4. Genesis, *The Pentateuch* , 29:17, Rashi p. 286. Genesis II, *Midrash Rabbah* II, 3rd ed. Trans. Rabbi H. Freedman (London: The Soncino Press, 1983), pp. 649–650. "*Baba Bathra*," *Nezikin* II, trans. Israel W. Slotki (London: The Soncino Press, 1935), pp. 510–511.

5. Genesis, *The Pentateuch*, 29:32ff. Genesis II, *Midrash Rabba* II, p. 653.

6. Genesis II, *Midrash Rabba* II, p. 653.

to be validated by others. Generally we find that the very qualities that can bring about redemption, that can redirect those who stumble on the wrong paths, are often ignored, mocked, demeaned. Little wonder that women long for validation. However, women of the Torah say and do things that are not validated, that they do not expect to be validated.[7] Sarah could not have expected her dear husband to look with favor at her strong insistence that he send his firstborn son, Ishmael, away. Rebecca could not be certain that Isaac would favor the ruse that took away his desire to give the worldly blessing to Esau. And Leah must have anticipated the dislike with which Jacob would greet her the morning after the marriage.

In short we learn from Leah that perseverance may join humility that goes with a readiness for gratitude, and thanksgiving and the courage to act in ways that may not foster validation from those we respect and love.

A poignant note that dramatizes the relationship between Jacob and Leah is the image he had of her sister, Rachel. She was beautiful; her attractiveness of face and form revealed her saintly character and won him over at once. We may infer that merely looking at her filled him with deep pleasure. Beauty has held its magic through the ages. It has been called "God's handwriting." Contemporary ideas define beauty as that ethereal constant that topples empires, wins the hearts of the most hard-hearted men, and continues to enchant us though we fear it may be only skin deep.

BEAUTY: YESTERYEAR AND TODAY

When we think of Rachel or Queen Esther, the beauties of yesteryear, or the beauties today, what do we see? Is it a particular feature, a way of walking, a smile, an air of grace? It may be all of this, but essentially certain facial characteristics are associated with youth and good health: large eyes, high cheekbones, and a narrow jaw. These qualities transcend cultures: Both British and Japanese men and women rank these features as beautiful, whether found on Caucasian or Japanese women. Researchers conclude that "there are greater similarities than differences in cross-cultural judgments of

---

7. *New York Times* (March 21, 1994), p. A14.

facial attractiveness." The investigators attribute this to the fact that we have an innate mechanism that sees a certain geometry of the face as beautiful. The beautiful face is different from the average one, which does not exaggerate the three qualities we refer to: cheeks, eyes, and jaw. Of great interest is the finding that these features are ties, in actuality, to disease-resistance, health, fertility, and youth. Faces considered youthful and healthy-looking are those with full lips, large eyes, narrow jaw, and a lower face that is small in comparison to the upper face. "These attractive facial features may signal sexual maturity and fertility, emotional expressiveness or a 'cuteness' generalized from parental protectiveness toward young." Is it only adults who are smitten with this kind of beauty? No. It begins in infancy. The same research team found that infants as young as 2 months preferred to look at physically attractive faces. Infants 2 to 3 months old and another group 6 to 8 months of age tended to look longer at attractive faces than at unattractive ones, the attractive faces adhering to the qualities discussed above. The article concludes that the faces favored by the ancient Greeks and Egyptians, (we may add Israelites, from earlier or later periods) are still those favored today, a fact which keeps cosmetic companies and plastic surgeons in business.[8]

If symmetry is equal to beauty, what may cause symmetry? Is it our natural inheritance alone, taking eyes, for example, from one parent or even from a great-grandparent? Perhaps. Other researchers say that the tendency toward asymmetry (lack of beauty) may come from factors affecting the individual in the womb or egg such as: poor nutrition, unusual temperature conditions, pollution, increased maternal age, radioactivity, parasites, and disease microbes. While all these conditions have a negative connotation in the secular world, our understanding is that they are given to us by God for a reason unknown to us.[9]

MOTHERS CAN REASSURE OUR "LEAHS"

Children, particularly girls, born into a family in which they are not the beautiful ones often suffer. In our society, where outer beauty

8. *New York Times* (March 21, 1994), p. A14.
9. *Science Times* (February 8, 1994), p. C1.

is projected in every image of screen and print, young and ever-younger models staring at us as the ideal woman, women may feel intimidated. What can mothers do to reassure our "Leahs" that they have virtues and significance as did Leah, the unwanted wife? Let us look at why we have children. Some reasons are obvious, others less so:

1. Affiliation: to promote love and intimacy within the family.
2. Nurturance: to express one's nurturing qualities by offering this to our children.
3. Expectations: To ensure the continuation of our people, hoping that our children will develop the potentials given to them by God.
4. Identity: To ensure acceptance as an adult of maturity in our community.
5. Fun: To have fun with our children, understanding that they provide opportunities for experiencing creativity, novelty, and pleasure.
6. Competence: To be competent in our role as parents, knowing that all we do may help them grow and develop into persons of good character and commitments to what is right and just.
7. Security: To hope that when in need our children will be there for us, to assist if necessary. (The adult child helping aging parents is one example.)
8. Morality: To reflect the need for religion, and doing good for our community and society at large.
9. Transcendence: To know that there is someone who will carry on after our death, to transcend this life on earth, knowing that our values, firmly planted, will continue from generation to generation.
10. Destiny: The desire to have children is very strong in women.

These are some of the reasons that women give for wanting children. But beneath each declaration is a central theme: an innate desire and longing of most women to have children, whether there is a known reason or not. God in His infinite goodness puts this longing into women. Once a child is born, a feeling of deep joy and completion envelops the mother. It is no wonder that some of the most treasured paintings and writings exquisitely portray a mother's love for her child.

Since there is no choice in who is born, male or female, one or many, beautiful or unattractive, intelligent or limited, what does one do with a child who is one of the less beautiful in a family of two or more children? What is that child's inner experience? Said one woman:

> They called me "Pudge" meaning "pudgy." Even my best friends did, adding that they were "only kidding." When it was time to go shopping for Passover to buy new clothes, I didn't want to. My mother couldn't understand why. I told her that I didn't need new clothes, that I was teased enough with the old ones, that I hated school and everyone in it. My mother listened and seemed to understand, but her soothing took the form of telling me to ignore them. "They don't mean it," she would say. Or: "They're jealous because you're such a good student." Finally, when I insisted that I hated it all, she went to the principal, Mrs. Fisher. A kind lady, she told my mother what she had told me: The girls were just teasing. I should ignore it. At this age, girls do this kind of thing, and so on. But I couldn't forget. The pain stayed until, a few years later, thank God, the moth turned into a butterfly! Or so everyone said . . .

Reading about the Biblical women often stirs the desire in many to emulate them, if only for an hour. Who does not want to play Queen Esther? Robin did. As the roles were being handed out for the Purim play, Robin, who knew she was tall and imposing, if not the most beautiful student, longed to play the queen. She had been a dutiful student and won prizes for her fine essays. But she was not chosen. Her close friend, Manya, was. Manya had long, shiny blond hair and eyes like blue saucers. At nine, she was already a head turner. Robin expressed her longing:

> If only I could have been on stage for just a few minutes, how thrilled I would have been. All the parents were coming to see us in the play. But I had only a minor role, for about two seconds, and then out the door. Beauty evaded me. But now, happily married, with children of my own, I

am told by my husband that he loves me and I am beautiful. Still, sometimes that old feeling comes back. I run to look into the mirror, just for reassurance. Silly, but true. Perhaps some day I'll be truly free. I pray it should be so.

OUR SOCIETY'S OBSESSION WITH EXTERNAL BEAUTY

Our society's obsession with external beauty for women can be devastating. But we need not be overpowered. One woman resisted and overcame:

I thought beauty was everything. And so I tried hard to always look and be beautiful. Of course, when you are young, you never think of aging. But then, one day, it happened: I noticed signs of aging. I hate to admit it, but I was horrified. I recalled reading about a famous author, a truly remarkable woman living in France, who said in one of her fine writings that at age forty, when she looked into the mirror and found signs of aging in her face, she wanted to commit suicide. I was appalled and terrified of my reaction to my aging. I knew something drastic had to be done. But what? Calming myself, I did some careful reflection: Who among my female friends did I consider truly beautiful? The answer snapped at me. It was the women who had a certain look: an air of calm, peace, and tranquility, an ease about their presence. What did they have in common beyond this? The answer was right there: They were true believers. Never had I heard them doubt. Could this be the glue that connected their inner and outer beauty? I decided to test my theory. Approaching one of my close friends, Claire, I put it to her: How did she manage to project this total sense of ease, this queenly grace in her entire being? With candor I told her that I loved being with her, that she radiated such beauty that everyone felt it. She was not "Hollywood beautiful." Each feature was not in synchrony with its neighbor. Still, she exuded an almost ethereal impression without effort. At the same time, I experience her as real, not Polyannish. What was her secret? Claire blushed and hesitated, thanking me for my words and then she explained,

"While I don't see things through rose-colored glasses, I feel positive about life and accept the flaws in all of us, especially in myself. But I know there is a reason for everything, and I don't stay negative for more than a split second, if that much. I have faith. And I trust." I asked her to explain. "Faith is to know that God is taking care of everything. Trust is to know that I can sleep in my bed at night, knowing that I will be taken care of." Claire continued, "Of course I have my job to do, too. God does what He needs to do, and I do what I need to do. It's like a good partnership where one is the outside partner and one the inside. Only here it's one above and one below. Working together, we get the job done."

I was struck by her words and the effortless way in which she expressed them. They seemed to come from some deep place inside of her, a hidden space with a long history. And then lightning struck. Was it that I could see and feel the inner beauty of Claire? Somehow, unbelievably, I had moved past the over-emphasis on external face and form, to the recognition of true beauty and its origin. I had developed new eyes. Now I could share a new way of being, my first baby steps, with others. And I would begin right here at home, reframing my ideas about beauty and putting them into action, especially with my daughters.

Can mothers help their female children to feel validated? Here are some ways in which we can validate a child's need for feeling beautiful and unconditionally loved:

1. Do not ignore or make light of your child's expressed feelings. Take them as real. Use words such as, "I understand your hurt. I have felt pain myself and it is not easy. Let us talk about things we can do to help you. Let's see what we can learn from what God is sending you. Once we see the message, we will be better able to do the right thing."
2. Every day, in every way, praise your child. If you must criticize, do it constructively. Offer an option. Make her feel good about herself. Instead of saying, "You did poorly on this test," say, "You have done much better. Perhaps this was not your best day or subject. I know you will do well in the future. And your father and I are here to help you."

3. Stress the values in your home. Be direct and explicit about how character, kindness, and goodness of heart are qualities to be most valued. While helping her feel beautiful, point out that beauty is a transient thing. Youth and beauty are fleeting. In addition to telling her this, you must live it. Children learn not from what they hear but from what they see. Your home reflects your most profound values as you live them in everyday life.

4. Be consistent. Parents who change their ways and behavior tend to confuse their children. Fathers should be as consistent as mothers, and both parents should be joined in decision making and building their child's self-esteem. Disagreements about which path to take for the child should be discussed between the parents alone, never in front of a child.

5. Share your own experiences of growing up with your daughters. Tell them your problems or successes: Were you the youngest? Oldest? What was it like for you? Did you feel pretty? Unpretty? What happened? Who were some of your crucial mentors? Where did you gain courage, your sense of uniqueness, your faith?

Acting as guide, mentor, and loving parent, pointing out the virtues of the Biblical women, we can encourage our daughters to experience their own worth. Early and consistent validation of our female children will ensure that, in the later years, validation from others may no longer be so crucial. As descendants of Sarah, Rebecca, and Leah, we carry potentials within that exceed our imagination!

❦ 4 ❧

Rachel: In The Spirit
Of Compassion

When mentioned at all, courtships in the Torah are not roman-
ticized. Abraham did not even know that his bride was beautiful, probably one of the most beautiful women in the world. Isaac
married Rebecca and *then* he loved her. Jacob was tricked into marrying Leah; not until she had borne him four sons did he come to
appreciate her worth. And in our study of more than fourteen other
women in this book courtship is not even considered.[1]

In contrast, Jacob meets Rachel at the well. She is a shepherd-
ess, herding sheep. At once, in order to water the flock that she tends,
he rolls the heavy stone from the well. He kisses her. Within one
month, he agrees to work for her father for seven years: "I will serve
thee seven years for Rachel thy younger daughter." Rachel, we are
told, was beautiful in form and appearance. "And Jacob loved
Rachel." The seven years he toiled for Laban seemed like a few days
"for the love he had to her." In the course of their marriage, Rachel
comes to envy her sister Leah who bears son after son while Rachel
remains barren. As a result, Rachel speaks to Jacob: "Give me children, if not I am a dead woman." Angered, Jacob replies, "Am I in

---

1. Genesis, *The Pentateuch and Rashi's Commentary*, trans. Rabbi
Abraham Ben Isaiah and Rabbi Benjamin Sharfman (Brooklyn, NY: S. S.
& R. Publishing Company, 1949), 12:11 and Rashi pp. 105–106. Genesis,
The Pentateuch, 24: 67; Genesis II; *Midrash Rabah* II, third ed. Trans. Rabbi
H. Freedman (London: The Soncino Press, 1983), pp. 657–658.

God's stead, who hath withheld from thee the fruit of the womb?"
In response, Rachel gives her maid-sister Bilhah to be his wife;
Bilhah conceives two of his sons. Further, Rachel gives her sister
Leah an extra night with Jacob in return for mandrakes, fertility
plants, which were given to Leah by her loving son, Reuben.[2]

In time, Rachel gives birth to Joseph and later dies in childbirth
with her second son, Benjamin.[3]

RACHEL AS THE ESSENTIAL FEMININE WOMAN

Rachel may be the essential feminine woman, standing out among
many women in the Torah. She is kind and self-sacrificing. Her spirit
of compassion is extraordinary. While desperate to become a mother
and envious of her sister Leah, she exhibits spontaneous feelings
of affection, concern, and a sense of connection. Rachel is able to
say that Leah must be able to bear so many children because of
her unusual righteousness.[4] Rachel's sterling qualities are difficult
to detect when we rely on the biblical text alone. Instead, we turn
to the Midrash to discover that Rachel accomplishes what Abraham,
Isaac, Jacob, and Moses cannot do.

RACHEL SPEAKS

When the temple was destroyed, God in great anguish asked
Jeremiah to summon Abraham, Isaac, Jacob, and Moses from their
sepulchres "for they know how to weep." When their spirits appear
before Him and plead for His mercy, He remains silent. Then Rachel
"broke forth into speech":

---

2. Genesis. *The Pentateuch*, 29:10–20 and 30:1–8. Quotations: 29: 18,
20 and 30:1–2.

"Rachel was very much a person whose self-expression took place in
the revealed world. . . . Her spirit could penetrate the multilayered con-
cealment that is inherent to the 'outer' world." Rebbetzin Tziporah Heller,
"Reaching our True Destination," *Hamodia* (July 9, 1999), p. 65.

3. Genesis, *The Pentateuch*, 35:16–20.

4. Genesis, *The Pentateuch*, 30:1–2; Rashi pp. 291–292. Genesis II,
Midrash Rabbah II, third ed., p. 657.

Sovereign of the Universe, it is revealed before Thee that Thy servant Jacob loved me exceedingly and toiled for my father on my behalf seven years. When those seven years were completed and the time arrived for my marriage with my husband, my father planned to substitute another for me to wed my husband for the sake of my sister. It was very hard for me, because the plot was known to me and I disclosed it to my husband, and I gave him a sign whereby he could distinguish between me and my sister, so that my father should not be able to make the substitution. After that I relented, suppressed my desire, and had pity upon my sister that she should not be exposed to shame. In the evening, they substituted my sister for me with my husband and I delivered over to my sister all the signs which I had arranged with my husband so that he should think that she was Rachel. More than that, I went beneath the bed upon which he lay with my sister, and when he spoke to her, she remained silent and I made all the replies in order that he should not recognize my sister's voice. I did her a kindness, was not jealous of her, and did not expose her to shame. And if I, a creature of flesh and blood, formed of dust and ashes, was not envious of my rival and did not expose her to shame and contempt, why shouldst Thou, a King Who liveth eternally and art merciful, be jealous of idolatry in which there is no reality, and exile my children and let them be slain by the sword, and the enemies have done with them as they wished!

"Forthwith the mercy of the Holy One, blessed be He, was stirred, and He said, 'For thy sake, Rachel, I will restore Israel to their place'."[5]

If we look carefully at Rachel's words, we come to see the great attention given by the Torah to the woman's voice as different from the man's, not in tone alone but in words as well. The references made by Rachel to her experience in saving her sister from shame are clothed in warmth and beauty, not a grand or abstract beauty

---

5. "Lamentations," *Midrash Rabbah* VII, third ed., trans. A. Cohen (London: The Soncino Press, 1983), pp. 48–49.

but a beauty that sparkles with the breath of the everyday encounters every woman can understand.

Rachel is being personal with God; there is a relationship here; she could well be speaking to a dear friend. And a dear friend would reverberate to the heartbeat of the words of Rachel. Is Rachel wordy? Yes, with words that reveal and relive her experience all the way to the smallest of details. Are we surprised that God, Master of the Universe, Master of all Creation, is listening to her, hearing her, and acceding to her wishes? Is God offering mankind a model to be emulated by every Jewish husband, brother, and son? "Listen to the voice of Sarah" is now magnified to "Listen to the voice of the woman. When she speaks in ways that may not be familiar to you, open your ears and your hearts and redemption will come."

WOMEN ARE DIFFERENT FROM MEN

Women are different from men. These differences go back to the first day of birth; inherent in each sex are certain genetically determined hormonal differences that govern behavior. The y chromosome contains a single gene that determines maleness. This gene signals a complex cascade of actions without which all human embryos would develop into females. Behavioral differences are seen soon after birth: Boys run for the toy trucks and cars, girls are attracted to dolls and play "house." Even when parents of very young children pressed baseballs into their daughters' hands and gave boys sewing lessons, given free choice, girls vied for dollhouses and boys climbed trees. Differences seem to be an innate given.[6] Most significant are the studies supporting the idea that women are more adept at reading the emotions of others than are men. Men and women, it is said, perceive the world in different ways. Males, for example, excel at rotating three-dimensional objects in their head. Women prove better at reading emotions of people in photographs. Shown pictures of actors portraying various feelings, women outscored men in identifying the correct emotion. Women, it is said, can dig beneath the word content and come up with the level of feeling underneath. The woman thus works on two levels: she hears the word *and* automatically

---

6. Walter Johnson and Marcella Bakur Weiner, "Sex Differences and the Brain," *To Your Health*, VI:2 (February–March 1994), pp.1–2.

associates it with a feeling. This appears to be an innate skill for women.

We can say that in choosing her words a woman really uses her head. For both sexes, the principal language centers of the brain are concentrated in the left hemisphere, but women use both sides of their brain during even the simplest verbal task, such as spelling. Woman's appreciation of everyday speech appears to be enriched by input from various cerebral regions, including those that control vision and feelings. This may explain why girls usually begin speaking earlier than boys, enunciate more clearly as toddlers, and develop a larger vocabulary.[7]

If women possess an innate ability to read other people's hidden motives and meanings, it follows that they are also sensitive to their own emotional context. Being in touch with their feelings, they can make conscious choices as to which emotional response seems appropriate at a particular time. This differs from feeling a surge of chaotic emotions that seem to have their own voice, over which a person feels little control. Having control means that women are aware of their inner world, can name emotional components readily, make conscious choices, take action accordingly, and take full responsibility as well.

If Rachel is the essential feminine woman, how ironic that the man who loved her so deeply could not fulfill her need to be cherished, and he could not offer her protection when in anguish she pleads for his help, "Give me children, if not I am a dead woman." Instead of protection, his anger is aroused against her.[8] Can we dare to suggest that, while presenting Rachel as the most compassionate and self-sacrificing of all heroines, the Torah alerts us to the extreme vulnerability of the very feminine woman? Her potential for bonding with others, in joy or in sadness, embraces a deep desire to be cherished. Unlike masculine energy that initiates and leads, feminine energy prefers generally to surrender to another, to receive, to be protected. Do compassion and vulnerability go together? We think yes. Compassion is the overt layer, usually expressed in acts

---

7. Christine Gorman, "Sizing Up the Sexes, *Time* (January, 1991), pp. 42–49.

8. Genesis, *The Pentateuch*, 30:1–2.

of kindness, a reaching out, an ability to be empathic, or to feel what it's like in the other person's shoes. It is a most admirable trait, and we veer toward such people in droves. But hidden within the folds of compassion is raw vulnerability. It is this very capacity to be open and willingness to risk that connects us deeply to our humanness. Sometimes this vulnerability lies concealed. At other times it gushes forward, revealing our susceptibility to hurt, pain, shame, or rejection, and the awareness that perhaps this one time we made the mistake of being too compassionate, too available, and too willing to be exposed. We shall come to see as well that like Rachel, Tamar, Jael, Abigail, and Esther draw momentarily on their own masculine energies when needed, when the significant men in their lives cannot, or will not take the lead. We shall see, however, that once the need has been met, these same women revert to their feminine natures and roles: nurturing, bonding, and caring patiently for others. They become helpmates again to provide and to do what men by nature cannot and need not be doing.

PAULA AND RALPH: A CONTEMPORARY COUPLE

Paula and Ralph, a long-married couple, were now retired and living a peaceful, happy life. The evening was a typical one. Ralph was organizing data for his taxes and Paula was reading. With time on her hands, eager to learn, she was taking some adult classes. It was close to bedtime when there was a sharp knock on the door. Ralph looked up: "Are you expecting anyone?" "No," answered Paula. "Are you?" Ralph went to open the door, thinking that this could be a neighbor. At the door, a middle-aged man, shirt askew, stood wringing his hands. Close to weeping, he pleaded, "I'm so sorry, so very sorry to disturb you, dear neighbors. But I didn't know where to go or whom to ask." Paula and Ralph looked at one another as the man poured out a flood of words: "My wife, she just had another seizure. I must get her some medicine right away or she may die. I have no cash in the house. It's Sunday and all the banks are closed. The drug store won't take my check. They say they've seen too much fraud. I need fifty dollars for the medicine. Please. I will pay you back first thing tomorrow morning. You will get your money." Caught in this torrent of verbiage, Ralph paused for a moment and asked, "Excuse me, sir, but who are you?" "Me?

Why, I'm your new neighbor. I just moved into the apartment below you. I knew you were awake because a few minutes ago, I heard you walk across your rooms. I'm sorry. I should have introduced myself, but . . . my wife . . . I'm so upset, I can't think straight." Ralph and Paula locked eyes. As with many couples who know one another well, Paula signaled with her eyes. Yes, indeed, he should give the man money. "I'll get you your fifty dollars," Ralph said. "Thank you, thank you," said the man. "But, just in case the medicine is a little more, could you make it eighty? You'll get it all back tomorrow, first thing in the morning." The exchange was made. The stranger thanked him and disappeared into the night.

Ralph and Paula never saw the man or their money again. A loving couple, neither one berated the other. There was no "You made me do it." But for Paula, there was a nagging feeling she could not shake off. Ralph was more dismissive: "It was a mistake. I should have known better. But how could I? There was not time to check him out; I couldn't go banging on the neighbors' doors at this time of night. He seemed so upset. And there was always this terrible thought that if we didn't give him the money, his wife might die."

In this case, a true story, some hesitations and checking would have been best, but not at the risk of giving up on compassion. Compassion is part of our spiritual life. While related to kindness, it is different. True compassion is the ability to feel empathic toward another because we too have been there. It is more than just a kind act. It is a way of connecting and delivering us from our own experiences of pain. In giving to others, we free ourselves. And, in accepting, perhaps welcoming our vulnerability, we take our chances. We get involved. We enter into relationships. We do not stand idly by in the face of cruelty or terror. Every human being counts. As we extend our compassion, we move closer to God. God cares about how we act toward one another, which explains why He gave us the commandments, a prescription for daily living.

COMPASSION IS PART OF OUR SPIRITUAL LIFE

Rachel is compassionate toward Leah but with true honesty, acknowledges her envy. She is barren, seemingly hopelessly so. Her sister is fertile, the fertility so prized. With two contrary emotions, Rachel gives top priority to compassion. That is a hard act to duplicate. When we see a child in pain, we rush to help. Who has not been in pain as a child, emotionally or physically? It is a familiar experience we can lock into. And we do. But what if the experience is an unfamiliar one? Can we still offer compassion?

We see a homeless person. They usually look ill kempt. If they approach us, we feel them intruding into our world. For many, the first response is disgust—"Why is this person, whom I neither know nor am concerned about, bothering me?" Our compassion leaving, we lose our humanity. Whether or not we choose to give to them, we do not even acknowledge them. We do not say, "I'm sorry. I am not giving," but instead, we look past them. We have relinquished our humanity. Rachel enriches hers. Despite her jealousy, she was able to honor her sister and save her from shame. She and Leah formed a sisterhood long before the word was coined.

Women have always bonded. As children, girls have a best friend, and often a second best friend or a third. This continues for a lifetime. Friends may change or die, but another is found with whom to bond. The best friend is now called a "confidante." Women who do well in life, staying healthy and happy, have one. Men have one, too. It is their wife if they are married and a woman friend if they are not. Both men and women often choose another woman with whom to share their innermost world.

No doubt confidantes, women bonding together expect compassion from each other. Leah must have had some idea that Rachel, her sister, would extend compassion to her in her dire situation. On some level, Rachel must have experienced the shame Leah might have suffered. Leah, too, understood Rachel's misery were she to have only one son.

MINDY FRAGMENTING

Mindy was fragmenting. Her world was falling apart, and she was trying desperately to keep some sense of wholeness. She had been betrayed. She feared a truth that was intolerable. Her husband had been having an affair. She had suspected this for some time, but when she raised the issue, she was quickly disarmed. She was "imagining it" or "had a suspicious nature due to earlier childhood experiences around her father." Life together became better than before. Until the tragic night, when looking through the pockets before taking his suit to the cleaner's, she found a note, "I long for you . . .", and a bill for an expensive piece of jewelry with another woman's name on it. Her world collapsed. She did what most women do under these circumstances: She called a close woman friend. She and Ellen had gone to college together, shared dates, and still giggled over the years they had "sleepovers" at one another's house. Now both were married with children. Ellen was emotionally secure, thought Mindy. Ever since college, she had turned to her for help and Ellen had always bailed her out.

> I don't know what I was looking for except that she would soothe me as she always had in the past. Boy, was I in for a surprise. There I was, sobbing and talking at the same time, spilling my guts, and Ellen said not a word. In fact, she seemed to be barely listening. Though I could hear her breathing, I felt she was a million miles away. Finally, I could stand it no longer. "Ellen, are you there? Do you hear me?" I was near hysteria by then. Ellen was calm, too calm. It was as though she was totally untouched. Nothing had gone in, not me, not my pain, not my story. She might as well have been reading some tawdry tabloid newspaper. But this was me, her very best friend. And it was my agony I was talking about. When she did speak, she was about as reassuring as a snakebite. She told me that everyone but me had known about it, and why had I not seen it coming? And then she dropped the boomerang, telling me that she thought my marriage had never really been any good, that we were very different types, that he was much more spiritual than I, and that this was the best thing that could have happened. We could now go our separate ways and begin all over again. She was dissecting my marriage in a cool, detached, cryptically clinical way. Feelings, mine or hers, had no place here. I was devastated.

Instead of offering Mindy nurturance, support, and reassurance, Ellen pushed her away. For some reason Mindy's situation made her uncomfortable. It tapped into issues in her life she did not wish to handle. Centered in her own pain, she was unable to reach out to another. Even when that other was a friend as close to her as Mindy. Her crisis was more than Ellen could handle.

Not everyone is adept at being empathic to all who are in need. Some women offer empathy only to the most significant people in their lives, such as close family members. Still others can be empathic to many different women but not at all times. Depending on their ability to be clear in their hearts, not allowing the debris of their own lives to cause overload so that they cannot reach out, they can give, but judiciously.

Perhaps, in order to emulate Rachel, we need first to reach toward that closest of "friends": God. It is likely that, as in the case of Rachel, through this divine connection, we will be free to reach toward others with hearts brimming with compassion. It may be that only then will we choose wisely those who extend this same divine gift of compassion toward us.

With the vision of Rachel and her sister, Leah, in mind we may value, in a new light, the stories of women like Tamar, Naomi, and Hannah—women who had to move for a time beyond their very feminine dependence—and the stories of others like Zipporah, Miriam, Deborah, Jael, and Abigail—who model the ability to act with great fortitude and independence when the men in their lives are unable or unwilling to take the initiative, and, when the crisis has passed, revert to their softer feminine selves.

ᗤ 5 ᗧ

Tamar: Never To Shame Another

In Chapter 38 of the Book of Genesis, Judah falls out of favor with his brothers who blame him for not urging them to return Joseph to their father. As a result he leaves them, marries, and has three sons. Judah marries the oldest one to a woman named Tamar, but because the son is wicked, he dies. The second son marries Tamar, is also wicked, and dies.

Like Rachel, Tamar appears to be a passive woman, one who can surrender herself to not one but two husbands without complaint, as each one dies by the hand of the Almighty. Having behaved poorly as husbands, these men were not deserving of life. Unlike the excessive mourning by Jacob when shown the blood-stained garment of his beloved son Joseph, the husbands of Tamar are not mourned. This contrast of juxtaposed themes marks further contradictions between Judah's failure and Tamar's success.

TAMAR, SILENT AND DOCILE

Initially, in the face of all that happens to her, the marriages arranged by her father-in-law and the deaths of her husbands, Tamar remains silent and docile. She continues subdued even when Judah, her father-in-law, tells her to return to the home of her own father: "'Remain a widow in thy father's house, till Shelah my son (the third

47

son) be grown up'. . . . And Tamar went and dwelt in her father's house," awaiting the marriage that would never occur.[1]

The story of Judah and Tamar follows the sale of Joseph into slavery and his term as slave to Potiphar. The wife of Potiphar yearns for Joseph. When rejected, she accuses him of seducing her. In contrast to Potiphar's wife, Tamar, also rejected, risks her own life rather than cause shame to Judah. Prior to the story of Tamar, Judah was instrumental in having Joseph sold into slavery, also in having Joseph's bloodstained garment shown to his father. After the sale of Joseph, "Judah went down from his brothers" and married a woman who bore him three sons before she died. That "Judah went down" tells us that his brothers removed him from the rank of highest son destined to be the ancestor of the Messiah. When they saw the grief of their father, they said, "You said to sell him. Had you said to return him we would have listened to you."[2]

TAMAR TAKES ACTION

The story shifts to its central theme when Tamar is told that Judah, now a widower comforted for the death of his wife, has gone up to Timnah to shear his sheep. The shift is marked by the sudden swiftness with which Tamar prepares to take action: she "put off" her widow's garments, "covered" herself with her veil, "wrapped" herself, and sat by the way of Timnah, "for she saw that Shelah was grown up and she was not given unto him to wife." Commentaries differ on whether Tamar planned to appear as a temple prostitute to lure Judah,

---

1. Genesis, *The Pentateuch and Rashi's Commentary*, trans. Rabbi Abraham Ben Isaiah and Rabbi Benjamin Sharfman (Brooklyn, NY: SS & R Publishing Company, 1949), 38:11–12, 15. Judah should have brought Tamar into his household when his wife died: "Bereishis"; *Sforno, Commentary on the Torah*, trans. Rabbi Raphael Pelcovitz, (Brooklyn, NY: Artscroll Mesorah Publications, 1987), p.185. On 38:15, "Because of her vexed expression, Judah did not like her," Targum Yonasan quoted in Yishai Chasidah, *Encyclopedia of Biblical Personalities* (Jerusalem: Shaar Press, 1994), p. 529.

2. Genesis, *The Pentateuch*, 38:1, Rashi note p. 382. "Genesis II," *Midrash Rabbah II* third ed., trans. Rabbi H. Freedman (London: The Soncino Press, 1983), pp. 790ff.

or whether she went to meet him to remind him of his promise to give his third son in marriage to her. When Judah, not recognizing her as his daughter-in-law, longs to have sex with her, she accepts the opportunity to fulfill the divine desire that she couple with a member of Judah's family, this time with the father himself.[3]

GOD TRICKS THE NEGATIVE FORCE

How then does Tamar redeem Judah, saving him for his role as ancestor of the Messiah? First, she rapidly accepts her new role, changing from the silent submission and surrender of her feminine self to an assertive and daring woman who quickly clears the path to mate with Judah. It is said in the mystical tradition that God at times tricks the negative force that seeks to frustrate the success of those who are righteous, planting deep pits on their paths to block the advent of the Messiah. When Judah lusts for his own daughter-in-law, the negative force is fooled into thinking there is no hope that these two can become channels for divine energy. Once the way is cleared of negative intervention, success is rapid.[4]

There is also a second way in which Tamar redeems Judah, making it possible for him to rise higher than ever before. When Tamar becomes pregnant, Judah is informed that she "hath played the harlot and, moreover, behold she is with child by harlotry." His immediate response is "let her be burnt."[5]

At the time of their encounter on the way to Timnah, Tamar asked for a pledge that Judah would send her the payment of a goat, the pledge being his signet, cord, and staff, very valuable items. On the way to fulfill the cruel decree of Judah that she be burnt, Tamar

---

3. Genesis, *The Pentateuch*, 38:14. *"Sotah," Nashim 3, The Babylonian Talmud*, trans. Rabbi I. Epstein (London: The Soncino Press, 1978), pp. 47ff.

4. From the union of Judah and Tamar, the Messiah was to spring: "Genesis II," *Midrash Rabbah* II, third ed., trans. Rabbi H. Freedman (London: The Soncino Press, 1983), p.787, note 5. "Genesis," *Studies in the Weekly Parasha*, trans.Y.Nachshoni (Brooklyn, NY: Artscroll Mesorah Publications, 1988), pp. 236ff.

5. Genesis, *The Pentateuch*, 38:24. "Numbers II," *Midrash Rabbah* VI, 3rd ed., trans. Judah J. Slotki (London: The Soncino Press, 1983), p. 508.

uses these three items to reveal what has occurred between them, sending them with a note to Judah: "By the man, whose these are, am I with child. . . . Discern, I pray thee whose are these, the signet, and the cords and the staff?" After reading these words, a purified Judah stands up, now the perfect Biblical leader, true to his God, honest to his people, repentant to his woman, to publicly admit, "She is more righteous than I."[6]

THE REDEMPTION OF JUDAH

On one hand, some Rabbis look unfavorably at the relationship of Judah and Tamar as ancestors of David whose genealogy includes his "tainted descent" from Tamar and Judah. The union was a forbidden one. "Since she was of such distinguished descent, her forbidden union with Judah was all the more reprehensible." (It is said that she was a descendent of Shem, the son of Noah.)[7]

On the other hand, we are told that the incident of Judah and Tamar had no ignoble motive, that their two sons Perez and Zerah were both righteous.[8]

SHE IS MORE RIGHTEOUS THAN I

Both Tamar and Judah confess their deeds, she privately to Judah and he publicly to his entire community. Both confessed and were not ashamed. In the end "They inherited life in the next world." Because Judah saved three souls from the fire, Tamar and their two sons, God later delivered his three descendants from the fire: Hananiah, Mischael, and Azariah.[9]

---

6. Genesis, *The Pentateuch*, 38:25–26. "Numbers II," *Midrash Rabbah* VI, p. 508.

7. "Ruth," *Midrash Rabbah*, Vol. VIII, 3rd ed., trans. Rabbi L. Rabinowitz (London: The Soncino Press, 1983), p. 92, note 4.

8. "Genesis II," *Midrash Rabbah* 2, p. 562; *Zohar*, Vol. II, trans. Harry Sperling and Maurice Simon (London: The Soncino Press, 1934), p. 218.

9. "Numbers I," *Midrash Rabbah*, Vol. V, 3rd ed., trans.Judah J. Slotki (London: The Soncino Press, 1983), p. 272; "Numbers II," *Midrash Rabbah* VI, p. 508; "Exodus," *Midrash Rabbah*, Vol. III, trans. Rabbi S.M. Lehrman, p. 210.

IS JUDAH GIVEN THE CROWN?

When the question is asked, "Why did God give the crown to Judah; why did the royal house of David descend from Judah?" the answer is that he had dealt justly with Tamar. At that time, Isaac and Jacob, grandfather and father of Judah, as well as all his brothers, tried to screen Judah (hide the apparently shameful act), pleading that the signet and the cord might have been lost:

> but Judah recognized the place (the general circumstances) and said, "The thing is correct. She is more righteous than I . . ." For this, God made him a prince.[10]

It is taught that the shame of this world is nothing compared to the shame of standing before God in the world to come.

And so, not necessarily the only brave one of his brothers, Judah is given the crown. Rising beyond the passivity of the excessively feminine, Tamar has succeeded in preparing the way, making possible what seemed so impossible. We see her at first as a passive, silently submissive, wrongly treated woman, apparently helplessly depending on others, believed by some to represent the "ideal" Torah woman. But in rapid succession, Tamar takes the initiative. With courage and risks to reputation and life, she reverses the downward pull of Judah.

Like all Jewish women, Tamar serves as the "preparer." Whether it is renewal, rebirth, or new birth, a woman makes the inner work possible. She is the *ezer kinegdo* (help meet) with whom man can bring down the divine energy to fulfill his role in God's great plan.

Tamar, a seductress to carry out the divine plan, is a clever agent on both her own and God's behalf. What can we do when women we know become oppressed, disappointed, and disillusioned because promises are not kept? Do we listen to them, recognize their love, triumph, profound pain, and try to help them? Or do we condemn them, reassert their victimization and blame them for "letting it happen or making it happen?" Do we point the finger rather than looking past it toward the ultimate vision that can unfold? Often women, despite severe trauma, can move past it to become brave and spiritually evolved. While excruciating, suffering may lay

---

10. "Exodus," *Midrash Rabbah* Vol. III, p. 369.

the foundation for strength of character. God sends us what we can handle. And handle it women can do.

TINA'S STORY

Tina grew up with a widowed mother. Her father had died when she was six years old, and her mother had never considered remarrying or, since she lived a relatively isolated life, partaking in the community. When Tina was twelve, money was tight. Her mother, a lover of cats, hated to cut down on buying all she felt necessary to feed her cats. Often preferring them to her daughter, she devoted most of her time to the cats—or so it seemed to Tina. Feeling the pressure to bring in money, her mother accepted an offer from her sister-in-law's husband, a widower, to come and live with him and share the expenses. Arnold seemed a quiet, reserved, distant man, apparently harmless. At first preoccupied with his hobby, collecting rare stamps, he spent hours in his room attending to them. Seldom did the three dine together; they had different schedules. Tina, too, spent much time alone when not at school or visiting girlfriends. Rarely did anyone come to visit her since, embarrassed at the messiness of her house, she did not invite them. When she was twelve, her life exploded. Arnold made advances to her, and frightened, not knowing what to do, she allowed them. While the shame was devastating, her sense of humiliation and degradation kept her lips sealed. Finally, almost two years later, she made up her mind to tell all to her mother. She braced herself. Wondering in her troubled mind if there had been any evidence of the relationship known to her mother or, as she suspected, did her mother know and ignore it, she braced herself and took the leap. "Mama," she said, "I have something to tell you." She stood trying to choose words deliberately, words to show what her experience had been, although she knew that nothing could express what she had gone through. "Arnold has been coming into my room a few times each week for a long time now. He has . . . he has . . . he has been making love to me, real grown-up love. He told me that he does this because he likes me so much and that younger men will try that too someday, but I would be better off with him." Her mother's reaction was as though someone were pummeling her brain. "That's not possible. He's not that kind of man. It could not be. And, let me tell you, young lady, if it did happen, I can't blame him, only you. You must have seduced him. Women do that to men sometimes. How could you? Don't you know that's wrong? Haven't you learned that this is to take place only after marriage? Didn't I teach you anything? Now you're a soiled woman. No one will want you. Forget about marriage. That's never going to be. You've ruined your life, *and* mine. And, if you think he's going to marry you, forget it. He's twenty-five years older than you and a member of our family, though, thank God, not a blood relative." With that she walked away to stroke one of her many cats.

TINA FELT ANNIHILATED

Tina felt annihilated. Pieces of her were crumbling inside, bit by bit. She could not cry. She could not scream. She was the cry; she was the scream! All of her longed to shriek, to call out to God, to ask his forgiveness, and to ask Him to bless her and take her life. Crushed, she knew that she had to end the relationship with Arnold. She told him that her mother did not believe her. Arnold said nothing. He sat still for a very long time. The next day he announced that he was moving; there was something about a business offer he had in another city. Neither she nor her mother ever heard from him again.

Tina carried her shame with her for many years. Despite this, she did well at school and had relationships with many young women her age. Understanding what pain can do, she decided to become a nurse. She wanted to work in hospitals, particularly with patients who were handicapped or who suffered from some debilitating, long-standing illness. She earned her degrees and went to work, becoming one of the most caring of all nurses. Patients would say, "When Nurse Tina touches me, I get better. She has magic in her hands and touch." Eventually she met someone at work, a young intern. He was, she knew, interested in her and she in him. But it took many months before she felt free to tell him her story, knowing well that as a member of a community, virginity was important to him. But Simon was understanding. He saw her as a victim who deserved his empathy and care. He never blamed her, for he could see the truth. "I think your suffering made you a better person. I see how you treat others. Do you think you would be so compassionate if you had not suffered?" Like Tamar, Tina coupled with a family member, but while she violated standards, God, in His divine wisdom, helped her to develop into the kind of woman who was a gift to all who were sent to her.

LURING SOMEONE TAKES MANY FORMS

In Tina we hear of a woman taken advantage of, a young girl abused, not the seducer, but the seduced. There are times, however, when a woman needs to be "the seducer." Seduction is not always sexual. Luring someone can take many forms. Laura used an unusual form of seduction to win back her husband. This is her story:

> I was losing my husband. Not in the usual way. He's a good man, my Charlie. But he was paying too much attention to work, and our family life was going under. I knew he worked hard and long hours. Having a retail business in electronics is difficult these days. Everybody wants everything and they want it right now. And the competition is fierce. If you don't take care of things right away, you lose your customers. Charlie worked with his brothers; it was a family business, and he was proud of it and the way it was run. He was an honest man. That was one of the main things I loved about him. A good businessman, he was also a good human being. I trusted him. And he was a good father. But, lately, he was just not paying attention. The kids would come to him with something they wanted him to see in their homework and he would tell them he'd look at it later. But he never did. I would tell him I needed to talk to him about everyday things but he'd sit still for just a minute and then run off to make phone calls or take care of some business. And I'm sorry to say this, but it's the truth: our private life was suffering, too. I used to love our intimate hours together. It was not only the pleasures that a husband and wife give each other. It was time to talk, to be together, to share and feel close with each other and with God. Now he seemed too tired. I didn't know what to do. I did not want to offend him, yet there had to be some way I could get him back to the way things were. I thought about strange things like getting

dressed in a special way at bedtime to entice and excite him. But that seemed silly and not necessary. Certainly it was not my style. I would feel like some stranger had taken me over. It wasn't right. Then, in one moment, the answer came to me. What did he really love? He loved food. Charlie, not a heavy man, was an eater. He *noshed* day and night, sometimes the right kinds of food, sometimes the wrong kinds, but he liked to eat. But, for my man, eating was a passion, one of the highest pleasures of life. So, I thought to myself, I have to work around this passion. I devised a plan. I decided to try it out on a weekday evening because it didn't seem right to do anything much different on the Sabbath. It was Tuesday and he had just come home. The children had already eaten and, as always, I was waiting for him. "So," he said, in his usual style, "What's for dinner, Laura?" I smiled to myself, but all I said was, "Come and sit down and you'll see." Then I served him the first course, an appetizer. He ate it with the usual relish. Upon finishing, he pushed the plate away to a side, waiting for the next dish. In the past, I would bring it very quickly, knowing that he was hungry and loved his food. But this time was different. I said, "The dish is special. It took some time to make. Before it is eaten, it has to cook in a special sauce but only for a short while before it is served. Otherwise, the whole dish is not tasty." This was a small lie, but in our tradition, that is sometimes allowed, I know, to keep the family peace. And I was trying to keep more than the peace; I was trying to keep my husband. So, Charlie and I sat together and, while he waited for the so-called sauce to seep into the dish for more delicate flavoring, we talked. And talked. And talked. Knowing that his beloved food was coming kept him patient. Even when the phone rang, he let the answering machine take it. A short time later, I brought the food out, laughing to myself. It was good, really good. And, best of all, he never suspected. Then there were two other servings, and, again, I said we needed to wait. And we waited and talked. At one point, our son came into the room and asked his father to check the book report he needed to hand in to his teacher the next morning. Charlie did, taking time to explain what he needed to do. I could see the joy in my child's eyes; just talking to his papa made him feel so good. Finally, it was dessert time. As before, there was the wait and the talk, in that order. The meal took over an hour whereas normally he was finished in twenty minutes. It was wonderful: good food, good conversation, a family closeness. What could be better? Something had happened. A marriage that was becoming stale was refreshed. And that night, we were intimate in our old way, close, caring, giving each other time, knowing that the love we had for each other and for God would always be our bond.

And so, Laura, like Tamar, played the role of temptress, but in a novel way. And God, sending her the plan, let her play it out in her unique way.

Sometimes seduction takes the form of redeeming the man, helping him to rise to a higher level. It may take place between daughter and father. It did for this family.

ELIZABETH WAS AN ONLY CHILD

Elizabeth was an only child. Her father had lost his first family in the war. All she knew was that he had been born in Berlin, Germany, and spent some time in a concentration camp. Not until she was a teen-ager was it revealed to her that her father had been a *kapo*, a guard in the camp, a Jew in charge of other Jews. While Hans was a good father, he sometimes seemed far away, preoccupied, an eternal look of sadness in his eyes. When people he had known in Berlin before the war visited, he was edgy, fidgety, nervous. Hedy, her Austrian-born mother, explained that the war "had done something to him." Others were always asking him, "How could you be a *kapo*, Hans, you, a carpenter? What was it like?" They always added, "I'm not here to judge you. I don't know what I would have done in the same circumstances." But her father felt judged as did she and her mother, Hedy.

"MY FATHER WAS A CARPENTER, THE BEST"

Hans developed problems with his lungs. He needed another climate and was offered a job in another city, one with purer air. Since experienced carpenters were needed, the salary was good. They moved. The new neighbors formed a welcoming committee and planned a party for him and his family. On that day Hedy came down with a cold but suggested that Hans go to the party with Elizabeth. She was now a young woman, socially poised. They went. The new community gathered around Hans. A few noted the concentration camp markings. Said one, "So, Hans, I see you were in the camps. How did you survive? What was your job there?" Before Hans had a chance to respond, Elizabeth moved closer to him. She said, "My father was a carpenter. The best, just as he is my father— the very, very best." As Hans turned toward her, Elizabeth noticed a drop of moisture gathering in one of his eyes. Was it a tear? His face seemed transformed. Miraculously, the tight worry lines around his mouth, the pained look of despair in his eyes, and the tautness of his features, which were often in a state of constant contraction, now softened. His jaw relaxed, his face became handsome and young-looking. Gratitude, not fear, shining in his eyes, Hans clasped her hand and gently pressed it. Now, instead of being questioned about his war experiences, he was besieged, as a carpenter, with work offers. That night, after the party, when Hans asked if she wished to go right home, Elizabeth said, "No, papa. Let's walk. I like being alone with you under the stars. I feel so safe." They walked and walked, arms entwined for a long time. When Hedy greeted them at the door, she said, "Hans, you look happy. How was the party?" Looking directly at his daughter, he replied, "It was the best of my life." He paused. "It *was* my life—given back to me."

Seduction and the redeeming of another comes in many forms. Women can use their feminine creativity to decide just which form is appropriate!

II

Journeys

৩৬ 6 ৩১

Hagar: Turnaround,
Reversing One's Destiny

Writing about Tamar and her confrontation with Judah (see Chapter 5: "Tamar: Never to Shame Another"), Rebbetzin Heller tells us about Tamar's confrontation with Judah: "The risks she took to do what she knew was her only honest choice were immense. She could certainly picture herself abandoned, rejected, and humiliated. All the calculations that, no doubt, were part of the decision-making process that brought her to the cross-roads of her fateful encounter with Judah could have easily been reduced to the dust and ashes that populate the section of our hearts reserved for broken dreams."[1]

BEING COMFORTABLE IS NOT THE PRIMARY GOAL

There are women other than Tamar in the Bible who suffered some form of rejection and who did not allow themselves to be taken to the precipice of despair. When being comfortable stops being the primary goal and desire, despair is no longer an option. Despair, writes Rebbetzin Heller, is "an option we may at times find comfortable, but one that is never really honest."[2]

---

1. Rebbetzin Tziporah Heller, "The Light of Awareness," *Hamodia* (May 21, 1999), p.75.

2. Heller.

Who then are these women, and how did they respond to challenges in their lives that could well have brought them to the precipice of depression? They include Sarah, Rebecca, Leah, Rachel, Zipporah, Miriam, Ruth, Naomi, Jael, and Esther. In this chapter, we plan to focus on Hagar, the women in Egypt, and in particular, the daughters of Zelophehad.

HAGAR: THE PRINCESS DISCIPLE

In the very beginning of the history of the Jewish people, two remarkable people appear on the scene, eager and ready to reach for deep and continuous understanding of the meaning of life and the purpose of being human. They are called Sarai and Avram and, later, Sarah and Abraham. Growing up together in a godless world of idol worshipers, they refused to accept at face value what everyone else was saying. With a brilliant mind and an honest heart, Abraham worked out a theology that has become the foundation for the Jewish people. This means that about four thousand years ago, the discovery of one God and His relationship to His creations began to take root, thanks to two people very different from one another and therefore well matched for spiritual growth that was forever evolving. They are models not only for all who have descended from them, but for all of humankind then and now as well. Abraham worked out a theology using his mind, and Sarah understood all with her heart. Mind and heart worked together and God took note. This couple when married was to be the root of a new nation on earth, the Israelites, but without a child, there could be no future for the nation. Sarah, with full understanding of this dilemma, pleaded with her husband to marry her beloved student, Hagar. Details can be found in Chapter 1 titled Sarah: "The Ability to Say 'No'." We wish now to concentrate on Hagar herself. If we ever need to watch the strange dynamic of body and soul at war, we recommend a close look at Hagar. Not unlike all of us, she moves from expressing the lovable, warm, intelligent, and nurturing side of woman to lashing out in anger and spite to say the most hurtful things about her beloved teacher and mistress. To visitors coming to the home of Abraham and Sarah, she would cry out. "My mistress, Sarah, is not inwardly what she is outwardly. She appears a righteous woman, but she is not. For if she were righteous, why has she not conceived in so many years? Whereas I conceived in one night!"[3]

HAGAR COULD HAVE BECOME BITTER

The abrupt change in Hagar is clearly connected with external circumstances: She is now not only the servant and student of Sarah, but the second wife of the great Abraham as well. And so she haughtily asserts her superiority over her mistress using words as daggers. Like so many of us, the selfish, egotistical, animal side has come forth to blot out the soul. But the soul never leaves. Hagar is sent away. Sarah has seen and understood the dangers, and Abraham must listen to the advice of his first wife.[4] Hagar and her son, Ishmael, must leave. In the harsh desert, close to death, using up the food and water provided for them, Hagar leaves her son under a bush. Sobbing, anticipating his death, she walks away. An angel sent by God appears to console her: Ishmael will produce a great nation. A well appears and Hagar and her son are saved. They are not heard from for many years. Ishmael returns to attend his father's funeral. A changed man, he fully acknowledges the truth that Isaac is chosen by God to follow the traditions of Abraham and Sarah. Hagar, too, has returned to the kind and generous nature that brought her so close to Sarah many years before. When Sarah dies, it is Hagar, now named Keturah, who becomes the second wife of Abraham. She has relented and done *teshuva*, acknowledging her shortcomings and showing regret for her past behavior. She "perfumed herself with mitzvahs and good deeds," actually rising above her original level. She bound herself with conscious restraint to keep away from the promiscuity

---

3. "Genesis I," *Midrash Rabbah* I, 3rd ed., trans. Rabbi H. Freedman (London, New York: The Soncino Press, 1983), pp. 380ff; quotation p. 382.

4. Hagar leaves twice: *her* decision, Genesis, *The Pentateuch and Rashi's Commentary*, trans. Rabbi Abraham Ben Isaiah and Rabbi Benjamin Sharfman (Brooklyn, NY: S. S. & R. Publishing Company, 1949), 16:3–14; "sent away," Genesis, 21:9–21.

prevalent among the desert people at that time.[5] We might well say that her time with Sarah as teacher bore fruit. But we know that another foreign princess, Orpah, enjoyed a similar stay with an outstanding Jewish woman, Naomi, and returned nevertheless to a life of degradation. The choices are ours. Hagar could well have chosen to sink into bitterness, even hatred, thus deepening the arrogance and spitefulness that took over when she was in the tent of Sarah. Instead, she chose the path of good deeds and faith in a God Who is kind and merciful, whose justice comes from His great love of His Creations.

A SISTERHOOD OF HOPE;
THE WOMEN IN EGYPT

Long after the time of Abraham, Sarah, and Hagar, the Israelites had to descend to the land of Egypt. Welcomed there for many years, they were eventually enslaved by the Egyptians, sinking lower and lower on the ladder that Abraham and Sarah had scaled so well. In the course of the descent of this holy people, there came a time when the Jewish men relinquished all hope of freedom. Living like animals, without voice, or choice, the future blackened and despair took over. At the end of each day, each man lay down on the dirt, on sand, on stone, and stole whatever sleep he could find. No thoughts of family, of wives, of children. How did the women feel? Did they skirt the precipice of despair as well? No! Somehow they managed to form a sisterhood in which they shared their common problems and drew on both feelings and thought to attend to the dilemma. How many hours they must have spent, surely in tears and lamentation. Without their husbands, the future was indeed bleak. How could there ever be a Jewish nation? What had happened to God's great plan, to His promise to Abraham that his seed would populate the earth and serve as God's emissaries to man-

5. Abraham takes Hagar, whose name is changed to Keturah, as his wife after the death of Sarah, Genesis, *The Pentateuch* , 25:1. See also Genesis II, *Midrash Rabbah* II, third ed., trans Rabbi H. Freedman (London: The Soncino Press, 1983), pp. 541–543. Dr. Blema Feinstein, "Saga of the Princess-Disciple," *Bas Ayin* (December, 1996), pp. 40ff, esp. note 6, p. 43.

kind? Somewhere in their struggle to work through the terrible plight, ignored by their husbands, hated by the Egyptians who had once welcomed their ancestors, the women came to a solution. They would find food for their tired husbands, prepare and bring it to them wherever they were. They must have discussed with pleasure how they would manage this project, not knowing that God would provide the special fish that the women would be bringing to their men. The plan was successful. Depressed and exhausted as the men were, their women arrived with hope and with love. Once again there was new life, new hope for the future.[6] That God took careful notice we know because, much later, freed from slavery, the Israelites in the desert built a traveling temple, the *Mishkan*. Offerings were made by all, but the offerings of the women were treasured above all other offerings. Why? Because they offered their shining copper mirrors, the very mirrors used to beguile their tired husbands into new life. These mirrors, favored by God, were used to build the basins in which the priesthood had to wash hands and feet in preparation to enter the Holy of Holies to perform their priestly obligations.[7]

A PASSIONATE LOVE FOR ISRAEL

Before the Israelites were to cross over to the Holy Land, there had to be a great deal of preparation about the allocation of land to those who had left Egypt and survived the forty years in the desert. The men were being counted in preparation for the distribution of the Holy Land. But there were five daughters who had lost their father in the desert and had no brothers. They were therefore left without any share in Israel. Their names were Mahlah, Noah, Haglah, Milcah, and Tirzah. Certainly they had every reason to feel rejected and humiliated. But as wise and learned women, they put their heads together and developed a plan of action, based on very careful thought. They waited for the proper moment to approach Moses.

---

6. "Exodus," *Midrash Rabbah* III, third ed., trans. Rabbi S. M. Lehrman (London, New York: The Soncino Press, 1983), pp.14ff.

7. "Song of Songs," *Midrash Rabbah* IX, third ed., trans. Maurice Simon (London, New York: The Soncino Press, 1983), p. 212. Exodus, *The Pentateuch*, 38:8ff, Rashi pp. 458–459.

Knowing that some of the tribes were negotiating a portion east of the TrasJordan, they waited for the completion of this settlement; no way did they want to have land anywhere but in the Holy Land of Israel, and not east of it. Drawing on the female power of persuasion, they called forth the attribute of divine mercy:

> The compassion of the Omnipresent is not comparable to the compassion of human beings. A human being might have more compassion for males, but He whose word brought the world into being is different. His compassion is for both male and female—His compassion is for all.

God acknowledged their petition: "The daughters of Zelophehad speak properly. You shall surely give them a possession of inheritance among the brothers of their father. . . ."[8]

The five sisters knew that the land had to be conquered and settled; they were aware of the distrust of the tribes and cries of "Why is God bringing us to this land to die by the sword?" Their faith in God was strong and their choices were clear: all Israel must ultimately possess the land, and they had to be part of the possession. God agreed, Moses agreed, and an important law was clarified: women were to be included in the inheritance among their uncles, even when there were no brothers to share. Continuity was assured for fathers without sons.[9]

To quote the distinguished Rebbetzin Heller, "The more one gives articulation to the Godly soul—by letting the dispassionate process of thought "outshout" that of instinct—the closer we are to ultimate victory."[10]

---

8. Numbers 27:1–11, *The Chumash, The Stone Edition*, ed., Rabbi Nosson Scherman and others (Brooklyn, NY: Mesorah Publications, 1993), notes pp. 886–889. Numbers, *The Pentateuch*, Rashi notes pp. 287–291. "Numbers," *Ha'amek Davar interpreted by Nachshoni*; Studies in the Weekly Parshah (Brooklyn, NY: Mesorah Publications, 1989), pp.126ff. "*Baba Bathra*," *Nezikin 2*, trans. Israel W. Slotki (London: The Soncino Press, 1935), p. 490. Dr. Blema Feinstein, "A Passionate Love for Eretz Yisrael—the Daughters of Zelophehad, *Bas Ayin* (June, 1997), pp. 31ff.

9. Numbers, *The Pentateuch*, 14:3; 27:7. Baba Bathra, pp. 487–488.

10. Rebbetzin Heller, "The Light of Awareness."

WORDS CARELESSLY FLUNG

When do we in our contemporary society revert to instinct, to our animal nature, even though we have been given the divine gift of free will? When we are unaware that the physical world has been given to us so that we can exert our own powers of choice, not only in deeds but in words as well.[11]

Hagar's contemptuous "showing off" attitude to Sarah must have caused the latter great pain. Words carelessly flung at another, mocking, or using sarcasm can be acts of cruelty. We call this *loshon hora*, that which, while true, is hurtful and therefore prohibited.[12] When Hagar says that Sarah has not conceived in many years while *she* has, she is stating a truth. This and her vehement attack against her mistress, declaring that Sarah is not the kind of righteous woman she outwardly appears to be, is *loshon hora*.

Habitual gossips who cannot wait to strew bits and pieces of character-defaming information along their paths commit *loshon hora*. They do not wait to filter words before they are released. Words pour out of their mouths uncensored, raw, often causing immeasurable suffering. This may lead to the breakup of marriages, the termination of friendships, even to untimely deaths. While the speaker is uttering *loshon hora*, a serious transgression, listeners, too, are part of this process. In our society not only is *loshon hora* not marked as such, it is considered quite normative as well. TV comics achieve high ratings, flinging insults at guests and at those in the news. The most popular magazines are replete with information of a private, often defaming nature. Presidential elections are won or lost by what adversaries say about their opponents. And, in daily life "telling it like it is" and "letting it all hang out" are considered to be virtues. Totally disregarded is the need for caution, consideration, and understanding of the possible dire consequences of what one so easily flings from the tongue. Fortunately, there are those who learn from their mistakes. Fannie did.

---

11. Moshe Chaim Luzzato, *The Way of God* (Jerusalem and New York, 1983), p. 81.

12. Zelig Pliskin, *Guard Your Tongue* (New York: Bnay Yakov, 1998), p.13.

Fannie was an outgoing woman with high energy. Her parents, close to each other, were devoted to their daughter. As a child she loved to listen to stories told by her mother and five maternal aunts. However, with humorous stories of the past and anecdotes of the present, they would gossip, often in colorful language. Fannie would sit and drink it in. As with many children, she used this as a model for her own behavior. Highly verbal and articulate, she became fluent in this modality.

FANNIE GOSSIPS

As a young woman, Fannie secured a job in the administration offices of a local hospital. Bright and efficient, she was a good worker. But she gossiped endlessly: "Did you know that Patient X was brought to the floor where we had no beds because Dr. Y was having an affair with her and pulled strings?" Or, "The head nurse in Unit B is married to a man who is about to go to jail for thievery. Can you believe that?" On and on it went. "Do you know what I just heard about? . . ." Because she was telling what was true, Fannie was unaware that she was committing a transgression greater than idolatry, adultery, or murder.[13]

No one stopped her until one day, God in his infinite mercy opened a way out. Fannie's parents were about to celebrate their twenty-fifth wedding anniversary. Fannie and her husband, Saul, wished to give them a party. They put together a list of friends and relatives when Fannie said, "Saul, I would like to invite some of the women and their husbands with whom I work. I have been there now for three years." Saul agreed that it would be a good idea and it would give him a chance to know them. Fannie sat down and carefully wrote out the names of the twelve women to whom she felt closest. She sent invitations to all with a date for returns. The invites came back. Fannie opened each one and could not believe what she saw. Each and every co-worker said she could not attend. Underneath most were the words "Sorry" and some reason why they couldn't make it: another appointment, someone's illness, location was too far, could not get a baby-sitter; for some, no excuse, only a bleak "Sorry."

---

13. Luzzato, p. 31.

Fannie, the last invite in her hand, burst out sobbing. Saul ran to comfort her. Heaving sobs, she looked up at him, asking, "But why? I have been working with these women. How could they all have an excuse? What is the matter? What have I done?" Saul did not have an answer. All he could do was hold his wife and tell her how much he loved her. Indeed, he himself did not know the answer, but he did offer a solution: "Honey, why don't you ask one of the women? Someone you feel the closest to and whom you trust may be able to help you. Maybe there is something you should know. I am curious too."

Fannie composed herself. The next day, at work, she approached her friend Elka. Elka had listened to her and seemed to like her, but she too had said she could not attend the celebration. Holding back tears, struggling for control, Fannie presented the situation. Why was this happening? Did she not have friends and working allies here? Was she not a good person? Did she not do her work well? Was there something about her of which she was unaware? Would Elka please be honest and tell her?

ELKA EXPLAINS *LOSHON HORA*

Elka was candid: "Fannie, you are a good person, but you do have a major flaw. You gossip; we call it *loshon hora*. As you know, many of us working here are observant Jews. You too are Jewish, and I think you told me that your grandparents were observant. Speaking *loshon hora* means you are telling the truth, but it is a hurtful truth. You are violating thirty-one mitzvos, seventeen prohibitions, and fourteen positive commandments. All these have either a direct or indirect connection with *loshon hora*.[14] You should know this." Fannie was quiet for a long minute, then said, "Why didn't someone tell me, stop me?" Elka put her arms around Fannie, "We have tried. But you are unstoppable. When you begin your tales, it is a faucet that gushes without end. You seem to be on a high. It is as though you have taken a drug. You have seen some of our patients on drugs. Their behavior changes. That's how you appear to all of us here. We have discussed this among ourselves and wanted to help you, but each time we tried to interject something, to say we didn't want to hear it, that we were

---

14. Luzzato, p. 29.

too busy to listen, you went on no matter what, a flood of words without end. And you must realize that if I or Rose or Evelyn or any of us listen to you, we are also transgressing. We did not want to be in that position. I, personally, dear Fannie, do have another engagement. I must go to my nephew's bar mitzvah, but I don't know about the others. I do think you should know what I am telling you. I am trying to help." Fannie's face had lost its color. Her voice was barely a whisper: "Thank you. I did not know. It was something I thought everyone did. I saw it at home. What do you think I should do?" Elka said, "I know this wonderful woman who is a *rebbetzin* and a psychotherapist. She has an excellent reputation. I suggest you see her. She will get to the bottom of this and point the way for you to make changes." Fannie kissed Elka and hugged her warmly, replying, "I am very grateful to you. I will call the rebbetzin tomorrow."

Fannie shared her experience with her husband, Saul. He said, "I love you and have always seen your wonderful qualities. But I, too, was aware of this." He laughed. "Sometimes you tell me that I am too quiet. But, honey, it is hard for anyone to get in a word when you are holding court. I think it is an excellent idea that you get some help. And then maybe, just maybe, I can be more of a talker and you more of a listener. Now that would be a change."

Fannie did go and consult with *Rebbetzin* B. who not only went over the laws of *loshon hora* but also gave her insights on why she had such a need to gossip. She said Fannie had a lack of self-esteem. She became so outer-directed that her interior life had failed to develop. Silence terrified her; it was a cave with no exit. In order to feel connected to others, she had to "entertain." Otherwise she feared that she would not be liked. She did not know her inner world. Seeing others opened the reservoir; they became a captive audience, and, for Fannie, a connection to life. To sustain the friendships, she needed ever-new material. Otherwise, stale stories would render her performance unacceptable. She was the constant searcher for gossip that was new, exciting, titillating, and provocative. The *rebbetzin* gave her some suggestions that helped.

HELPFUL HINTS

1. Recognizing that God hears and knows everything, Fannie had to filter her words. The therapist used the analogy of an

orange, explaining that if one wanted to drink orange juice, the orange had to be strained. Using a strainer would eliminate the pits, pulp, and peel. In the same way humans need to use a "strainer" for their words. Not every thought needs to be expressed, nor every story repeated. It would, said the *rebbetzin*, be a matter of selection. The crucial determinant of what is said, or not, is deciding if what you are about to say is necessary—if it is to be used for a beneficial purpose.

2. Fannie, afraid of silence, had to learn to be quiet, which was the way to get to her true self, her true nature. While people are an important part of one's life, the ability to be alone, to think by oneself, or pray by oneself, is a prerequisite for healthy living. To do this, the Rebbetzin recommended that Fannie spend some time each day by herself, sometimes to sit quietly and contemplate, at other times, to pray. God would hear her prayers. And this would become her strongest connection, for God did not need to be entertained.

3. Fannie could learn to study Torah and the laws of *loshon hora* as well as her people's history and its laws. That would give her an in-depth understanding of her religion. She was invited to some of the Torah classes the *rebbetzin* was conducting. Books were suggested as a way of beginning her study.

4. Fannie was not to indulge in self-blame. Nor was she to feel that her mother and her aunts were not good people. They had flaws. All human beings do, but goodness is preeminent. Making a correction, changing one's ways, is a giant leap forward. God sees and hears all and rewards us.

5. Fannie could ask her husband, Saul, to help her in this transformation. When she felt on shaky ground, when she was unsure of whether she was breaking a commandment, he could help her. To do this, he would have to begin his own studying. That would be an additional bond between them, and since they were planning to have a family, they could carry on their tradition through their children.

6. Fannie could share this information with her women colleagues at the hospital and continue her friendships. Admiring her willingness to make changes within herself, the *rebbetzin* invited Fannie to some of her classes.

And so Fannie, like Hagar, did a complete turnaround, discovering and welcoming her kind and generous nature. Acknowledging her past mistakes, she went beyond them, elevating herself to a higher level. Choosing not to respond with anger to Elke's revelation, she, like Hagar, chose the path of good deeds and faith in God. Everything is decreed with the utmost precision according to what is truly best. Fannie learned this, believed it, and most critically, lived it. *Loshon hora* gradually lessened as Fannie's sense of self, connection with God, bonds with others, and ability to consciously select what she said increased. With a newly elevated sense of self, she could fulfill her true potential.

◖◗ 7 ◖◗

Miriam: Vessel Of Hope

When is hope not necessary? When the sun shines bright, flowers stand tall, and people can smile. When is hope most unlikely? In shame, in despair, in a dark, dark place of longing where we dare not confess the depths into which we are thrust. Yet only then is hope essential; only then can it be born.

In this light, we look into the texts that tell about the suffering in Egypt long, long ago. The ruler, Pharaoh, a proud and mighty man was determined to prove that he above all others was the god who created the Nile, the river that provided sustenance for the land. As their god, having to rise above human functions, he rose early each day, decreeing that no one leave his home before a certain time in the morning. The Pharaoh could then hurry to the river to take care of his bodily functions and thus conceal his nongodliness from all.[1]

---

1. Exodus, *The Pentateuch and Rashi's Commentary II*, trans. Rabbi Abraham Ben Isaiah and Rabbi Benjamin Sharfman (Brooklyn, NY: S. S. & R. Publishing Company, 1949), 7:14ff; Rashi note 7:15 p. 62. For a beautiful description of Miriam's spiritual legacy, see *Rebbetzin* Tzipporah Heller, "The Freedom To Be Ourselves," *Hamodia* (January 8, 1999), p. 53.

DEVASTATING DECREES

As god of the Nile, Pharaoh began putting other decrees into effect, which were gruesome and devastating to the Jewish people. He robbed them of their dignity, allowing them no time to take care of their bodily needs, sending them to catch repulsive insects and rodents, and forcing them to eat food with hands covered with filth. At the same time, Jews were burned on Egyptian altars, infants plastered into the bricks of structures created by the Jewish people, and Jewish boys tossed into the river to drown.[2]

A BABY GIRL IS BORN

The year the hateful decrees took effect, a baby girl was born to the leading family of the Jewish community. Her name was Miriam denoting the bitterness (*Mar*) that twisted the lives of her people, a bitterness that grew stronger and stronger, beginning with the year in which she was born. Nevertheless when the women referred to Miriam as "Bad Fortune," she replied that they should call her "Good Fortune" instead, since the harsher the subjugation, the closer at hand was the redemption. She reminded them that like a woman in childbirth, the closer the delivery, the worse the pains.[3]

When Miriam was 5 years old, she assisted her mother as midwife. The Pharaoh commanded the midwives to kill all Jewish boy babies at birth. Despite the decree, Miriam and her mother found ways to keep the babies alive, boys as well as girls. Birth in and of itself became a vital link between this world and the world beyond; those who become part of this linking are said to be lifting Israel to God. Miriam became known as "Puah" because she would revive (*mefi'ah*) the infant when others said it was dead. She even amused the babies by making bubbles of wine that she placed in her mouth. At the same time that she was lifting Israel to God, Miriam lifted

---

2. "Exodus," *Midrash Rabbah* III, third ed., trans. Rabbi S.M. Lehrman (London, New York: The Soncino Press, 1983), pp. 12–25. Rabbi Yaakov Culi, "Exodus I," *Me'Am Lo'Ez*, trans. Rabbi Aryeh Kaplan (New York, Jerusalem: Maznaim Publishing Company, 1978), Vol. 4, pp. 12ff, especially p. 15.

3. "Exodus," *Midrash Rabbah* III, p.17 note.

her face against the enemy saying, "Woe unto this man when God comes to exact his retribution." When the Pharaoh wanted to kill her for this, her mother (Yocheved, here called Shiphrah) reminded him that Puah was only a child who knew nothing. Yet nothing was further from the truth![4]

Pharaoh was not the only authority figure to be rebuked by Miriam. Her hope for a better future gave her the courage to stand up to her own father, Amram, head of the *Sanhedrin* in Egypt. When Pharaoh decreed that sons had to be killed, Amram separated from his wife, and the Israelites followed his lead. Miriam dared to compare her father to the Pharaoh:

> Your decree is more severe that that of Pharaoh; Pharaoh decreed only concerning the male children, and you decree upon males and females alike. Besides, Pharaoh being wicked, there is some doubt whether his decree will be fulfilled or not, but you are righteous and your decree will be fulfilled.

Amram, and then all the Israelites, took their wives back.[5]

MIRIAM: DARING IN THE FACE OF AUTHORITY

What we see in little Miriam is, without doubt, a courage, a daring in the face of authority, which is not necessarily rare in young people. More startling, however, accompanying her ability to continue to hope when all seemed lost, were the signs of maturity that can discriminate between right and wrong. Miriam knew when to display kindness to the helpless and when to stand firm and unyielding to the powerful when they erred.

Shortly after the birth of Moses, who was prophesied by Miriam to be the man to save Israel, the Egyptian killing crew arrived to take the baby away. The mother of Moses placed her son in a reed basket and set it afloat on the river. Despite the gloom in that home,

---

4. "Exodus," *Midrash Rabbah* III, pp.16–17.

5. "Exodus," *Midrash Rabbah* III, p.18. "*Sotah*," *Nashim* 3, *The Babylonian Talmud*, trans. Rabbi I. Epstein (London: The Soncino Press, 1978), p. 60.

it was Miriam who followed the basket, wanting to know not whether the boy would live, but what would be done to him. In short, she watched to see, not whether, but *how* he would live.[6]

As a result, Miriam was present when the Pharaoh's daughter, filled suddenly with the light of God, rescued the infant. With true insight and the ability to act at once with confidence, Miriam offered to bring the baby to one who would nurse him (Moses would not nurse at the breast of an Egyptian woman). Once again, Miriam saved the day, for she was free to take Moses back to his mother who nursed him until he was weaned and returned to the palace to be raised by Pharaoh's daughter.[7]

A LEADER OF WOMEN

During the departure from Egypt, Miriam, as leader of the women, "lifted a timbrel in her hand, and all the women went after her with timbrels and with dances." Leaving Egypt with musical instruments reflected the remarkable faith shown earlier by Miriam as the child who followed the baby Moses, cast adrift on the River Nile.[8]

As a woman, no longer the daring child, Miriam married Caleb and bore him Hur. Her great-grandson is said to have been born in the merit of her wisdom. He was Betzalel, chosen by God to build the *mishkan*, the tabernacle in the desert, because of his remarkable wisdom and brilliant mind capable of absorbing both abstract and practical wisdom. In addition he was a competent teacher who passed on his knowledge to others. It is said that this legacy was Miriam's reward for her earlier devotion. But Miriam's adult years were not without darkness and suffering. After the liberation from the slavery of Egypt, the Jewish people were awaiting the return of Moses who had ascended the mountain to receive the tablets from God. Having miscalculated the day of his return, they became fearful that he was gone forever. It was Hur, Miriam's son, who rebuked them for think-

---

6. "Megillah," *Mo'ed* 4, *The Babylonian Talmud*, trans. Maurice Simon (London: The Soncino Press, 1978), p. 82. Exodus, *The Pentateuch*, 15:20 and Rashi note, p.164. *Sotah, Nashim* 3, p. 65.

7. "Sotah," p. 64.

8. Exodus, *The Pentateuch*, 15:20ff; Rashi note, p.164.

ing Moses would not return. The ability to rebuke improper behavior had served his mother well, but it resulted in the death of her son, for when he tried to stop the worship of the calf, the people slew him. Because Hur risked his life for the glory of God, all who would descend from him were promised a great name in the world. Once again, Miriam is responsible for future good in the world.[9]

In the desert, Miriam was responsible for the water that flowed wherever the people journeyed. When she died, it was as if the hope that glowed forever in her heart could no longer lift the spirit of her people. In its place panic spread throughout the camp as soon as her people found the water gone. God told Moses then to listen to the people asking for water, go to the rock, and draw water with trust. In this way, God was hinting, Moses would pay the greatest respect possible to his sister, Miriam.[10]

It is said that no worm may touch the following: Abraham, Isaac, Jacob, Moses, Aaron, Benjamin, and Miriam. It is little wonder that all the virtuous women came to Miriam to gain knowledge of the Sovereign of the universe. "Happy is that generation above all other generations."[11]

Embodiment of the light of hope during the darkest of times, Miriam remains a teacher of women seeking knowledge of divine wisdom, the knowledge that brings true happiness.

The Torah teaches us that each person is born with certain limitations, as well as the tools that are necessary to surmount such challenges and, at times, even turn them into positive energies. The general environment into which Miriam was born was a bitter one. Yet we learn that hope can serve as the lever to light the darkness of the deepest pit.

Hope is an emotion, a feeling of optimism that wells up inside of us. Its source is God, its channel the soul.

---

9. Exodus, *The Pentateuch*, 1:21. "Exodus," *Midrash Rabbah* III, pp. 459ff, and pp. 549–550.

10. *Chukas*, 20:2ff, *The Chumash, The Stone Edition*, Artscroll Series, trans. Rabbi Nosson Scherman (Brooklyn, NY; Mesorah Publications, n.d.), p. 843 notes.

11. "*Baba Bathra*," Nezikin 2, *The Babylonian Talmud*, trans. Rabbi I. Epstein (London: The Soncino Press, 1935), p. 86.

RELIEVING "ANGST," HOPE CAN SURFACE

With Pharaoh's decree that all baby boys be drowned, there was a small likelihood that Moses would be saved. But, despite uncertainty and anxiety, hope can surface, relieving "angst" and motivating one to push ahead. Thus, committed to the task of serving God, Miriam stood firm. She was an optimist par excellence, using her positive sense of hope to shift darkness into light. Not an end in itself, hope is an inspirational way station toward deeply felt long-range commitments.

No emotion exists by itself. It rides alongside and merges with motivation and thinking or cognition. Each feeds the other.

If a child sees dogs approaching and has been trained to fear them, she will retreat. But a child who has been with dogs and suffered no harm, and is told that dogs are friendly, will move toward and even pet the animals. Changing our thinking changes our way of responding emotionally. This can be learned early in the family of origin. Miriam learned in hers. At 5 years of age she was already hopeful, enthusiastic, eager to do what needed to be done, helping her mother with midwifery, saving babies considered dead. Thus, the preciousness of life, however short, was firmly planted in the mind of a young child. Miriam's early experiences prepared her for her mission as one of the three saviors of the Jewish people.

A PARTNERSHIP

A child learns to be a partner in the first year and a half of life. She interacts with the emotional tones of the parental figures, tones of love, admiration, control, and firmness. If a young child having difficulty trying to pick up something has a parent who nods and smiles in her direction, the child will feel masterful and hopeful that she will accomplish her task. The seeds of hope have been nurtured.

The very young child learns also by imitating what she sees around her. Miriam saw her mother performing midwifery. Brilliant and quick thinking, she began to imitate her mother. Even before the age of one year, an infant can imitate feelings and behaviors. Research has shown that a child only a few days old, facing a depressed adult, tends to withdraw and look depressed. The converse is also true: a smiling face leans toward her and there is the hint of a smiling response, correlate of hope. The world is the one young children see around them; with their agility for learning, children quickly take on that which they witness. Miriam took on what her mother, Yocheved, did. She learned to "copy Mommy." At the same time Miriam brought in her own unique talents. Yocheved beautified the newborn with lovely garments while Miriam sang to the babies. Her God-given talents were nurtured.

DEVELOPING ASSERTIVE BEHAVIOR, TAKING THE INITIATIVE

Closer to the age of 2, a child begins to use her behavior as a way of forming self-definition. No longer just copying, she is doing things to suit her own unique needs. Miriam had to have been an early self-starter. The sense of one's self as an initiator is a crucial attribute women can acquire if the groundwork is prepared early on. An initiator knows and feels that she can have her own needs met while, like Miriam, she works for the good of the many.

Another aspect of self-assertion is the development of curiosity, that insatiable hunger of children to know, to explore, to take a chance, to be an adventurer. How does it begin? To develop the freedom to be curious and explore, a child needs also to feel attached, not only by being held, rocked, sung to, and comforted, but also to know the parent is there, even from a distance. When Yocheved was not physically close, chances are that she communicated to Miriam that she could return for the hugs and kisses of reassurance. The secure child feels that, even when not near, the loving parent will return, at any moment, to give the soothing love that is so needed.

Miriam developed her creativity as well. Keeping Jewish baby boys alive even for a short time, until the Pharaoh's henchmen arrived, she amused the babies with bubbles of wine in her mouth. Imagine the bizarre scene: Miriam playing with babies in the face of possible annihilation and the Pharaoh wanting to kill her because of her precocious rebuke against his cruelty.

Miriam's strike against authority is a sign of self-assertion and inner security. Not only did she rebuke the Pharaoh, but she also took on a parenting role with her father, a leading figure in the

Sanhedrin. Convinced of the truth, she succeeded in having her father, Amram, rejoin his wife, whom he had divorced to avoid creating children who would be drowned. Miriam used her initiative by following her baby brother and then revealing to the Pharaoh's daughter, who rescued him, that she knew a woman who could nurse him. Miriam was truly the essence of unbounded hope.

How then can we help develop a child's feeling of hope? What styles of living can nourish a child's budding personality, and what behaviors can stifle them? Here are some examples from everyday life in the now.

PARENT TO THE PARENT

Trudy was a good, if very busy, mother. With three small children, she was always in a whirlwind of activity. To relieve herself, she turned to her oldest daughter, Essie, who was seven. "Essie," she would say, "I have to go to the store. Watch your little sister and brother." "But, Ma," Essie would complain, "I'm supposed to go over to Sally's house to study." Trudy would get upset. "I need you now. And I know you; you say you'll study, but the two of you will just play. Besides what's more important: your mother's health—you know how exhausted I am—playing with your friend?" Essie would give in and stay to mind her siblings. Chosen as the "dutiful daughter," her hopes for freedom from chores slowly began to vanish. When she told this to her mother and to her father, Max, both would say that life was hard, that daughters had to help out, and since she was the oldest, this was her job. When Essie pressed on, her father would come down hard: "Look, miss, we do things by the book in this house, and as long as you are living in my house, you'll do exactly what is asked of you." When Essie obeyed, her parents did not express their appreciation. They believed that she was simply doing what was necessary, no more and no less.

When a child feels burdened and is taken for granted, the sense of hope slowly fades. Reflecting the attitudes of her family, Essie saw life as difficult. Obligations needed to be fulfilled, leaving little or no time for play. Most hurtful of all was the feeling that her wishes were inconsequential. While hope within lay smoldering for a while, it would eventually go into hiding. As an adult, Essie would probably be a good woman, hard-working and conscientious. But hope and joy would not surface. Life would be interpreted as forced routine, with obligation as the major theme.

You may think that Trudy, the mother, was very busy and needed help. However, she could have sought to understand Essie's needs at each developmental level and matched the tasks to the stage. They could have negotiated. Trudy could have said, "Honey, I know you want to go to your friend's house, and I understand how important that is to you. I felt the same way when I was your age. But right now, I could use a little help. It would be so wonderful if my big girl could help out. Knowing that big sister is in charge for just a little while, I feel all will be well. If you run into trouble, you can go next door to Molly and she will come to the rescue."

The mother might well have added, "As a reward for your *chesed*, you could stay up a little later tonight and you and I could read that new book you brought home. Would you like that?"

This approach would acknowledge Essie's yearnings, move Trudy to re-connect to longings from her own childhood, and show her appreciation of Essie, joining her in an act of sharing that she and her daughter would enjoy. Thus, while the obligation would be fulfilled, Essie would learn that she was cared about, seen as her own person, and her needs, wishes, and feelings recognized. Hope would be kindled and life seen as offering a host of adventures with potential for unforeseen possibilities, the foundation of hope. Essie, feeling understood, could then develop her inner potential, with her soul nourished and hope restored.

LEARNING TO BE ASSERTIVE
IN THE THREE-PERSON SYSTEM

At times, your child's assertiveness is carried to an extreme. Her behavior becomes obnoxious, her grades are poor, her teachers complain that she is "acting out," and other children shun her. Your child seems confused. Unable to concentrate, she makes impulsive choices that are potentially harmful. Things, you think, seemed better when she was younger. But now that she is 8, she seems to be in turmoil, as are you, not knowing what to do. The house seems to be run by her, and you do not know how to stop it. You and your husband feel powerless.

When a household becomes chaotic, and children have no limits, it may be that the parents have difficulty with each other as well
as with their child. In all cases, parents must act as a unit. If you
say "No," and your husband says "Yes," each of you undermines
the other. Your child is caught in a web of pushes and pulls. Shall
she turn to one side or the other? Where is her allegiance? Will she
feel guilty if she ignores one of you and listens to the other? And,
most of all, what can she do with this overwhelming power that,
unrequested, has been bequeathed to her? Terrified, adrift in a web
of emotions beyond her comprehension, she moves strictly on impulse, anything to keep her busy. Constant movement prevents the
intrusion of thinking, for thoughts arouse logic and a sense of order. Space between thoughts, even between words, means quiet
time, a danger to be avoided. In her home of chaos, order is not
learned; a house divided is not in order. Where is hope in all of
this? Hope becomes distorted into immediate gratification, where
the "I want, I want" becomes master not only of the child but of the
household as well.

How can you change this? Most urgently, you need to set limits and mean it, show it in voice and action. Instead of quibbling,
you should use the energy to forcefully say "No," or "Not now," or
"Stop it." Setting limits allows you to fulfill your parental responsibilities, and it pulls your child out of the terror she is experiencing.
It shows her that there are adults in the household who know what
they are doing, mean what they say, and truly care about her enough
to squelch fears that terrorize her.

Fraida tried this. Her young daughter, Natalie, was a willful child
bent on having her way all the time, her anger instantaneous and
furious. This spilled over into actions: hitting another child, breaking something in the house or one of her own toys, yelling at her
parents, and sometimes holding her breath. Fraida, aware of these
behaviors, acted quickly. Firmly holding Natalie within her own
frame of vision, looking calmly into her eyes, quietly but firmly, in
a voice that was unshaken, she said "No." Staying near her daughter until this took effect, she showed that she, the mother, would
neither abandon Natalie nor let her spill out of control. After this,
some reward was offered and the incident dismissed. The lesson
having been learned, it could be put into the past and not conjured
up again.

Natalie learned that she could wait for what she wanted, that she could long for something and not feel annihilated if her yearnings were not immediately gratified. Not only does this build strong character, it also builds hope, the hope that what we yearn for may come about. If not, other things just as good and valuable may be sent. God can be trusted. With quiet restraint comes strong assertiveness. One is in control of the emotions, and feelings do not link with terror. Anger, when the world does not go the way one wants it to, shifts to acceptance. Beneath it all, the three-party system that dominated and separated the home can become a unit, a true family.

Miriam, though young, united her family. She must have realized that while her father, Amram, and her mother, Yocheved, had separated, they were not truly separate. Strong feelings of love bound them together, and Miriam could arouse them to reunite the family unit. Beneath it all, Miriam drew on the waters of hope that surged through her being. Hope can open a window in a dark world and allow the light of God to enter.

◖ 8 ◗

Zipporah: Courage In Crisis

Zipporah? Who is Zipporah? Well may we ask, for Zipporah is one of the most hidden of all women in Jewish writings. One must search diligently to discover her greatness. Her name is not listed in the index of Talmud (English translation). She appears in the Book of Exodus (2:16), but her name is not given until 2:21 where we learn that Reuel Yisro "gave Zipporah, his daughter, to Moses."[1]

As a Torah wife, Zipporah's behavior relates to a category found, not in the first Five Books (the *Chumash*), but much later in Judges and Prophets where women like Deborah, Jael, Hannah, and Abigail, at moments of crisis, take on tasks traditionally assigned to the men.

WOMEN WHO TEMPORARILY TAKE ON MEN'S ROLES

The prophetess Deborah urges Barak, her husband, to go to war against the powerful armies of Sisera who has conquered Israel. But Barak believes that unless Deborah joins them at war, his men will not follow. Unwilling to participate in war, Deborah nevertheless takes part in it, without actually fighting, for she knows it is God's

---

1. Exodus, *The Pentateuch and Rashi's Commentary*, II, trans. Rabbi Abraham Ben Isaiah and Rabbi Benjamin Sharfman (Brooklyln, NY: S. S. & R. Publishing Company, 1949), 2:16 and 2:21.

will that the war take place. We learn also that the final blow against the enemy is taken by Jael, a woman who resists killing with a sword, the way that men kill. Instead, she takes on a far more difficult task, as we will learn, and so protects her essential feminine self from becoming masculine.[2]

Later in the Book of Samuel, Hannah has been barren for eighteen years. Suddenly she realizes that her husband, who has been praying that she conceive, has lost hope. Although he seeks to reassure her that he loves her more than ten sons, she knows that her own prayers have become necessary. So intense and effective are her prayers, they have been taken by the rabbis as a model for the *Amidah* prayers of every Jew.[3]

Abigail, wife of Naval, a selfish and wicked man, remains a devoted wife until the day that David, prior to the ascension of his earthly throne, is maligned by her husband and, as a result, seeks to kill him. Realizing that killing her husband would hinder David's role as future king, Abigail takes the place of her husband as host and provides an enormous quantity of food for the four hundred men with David: two hundred loaves, two barrels of wine, five slaughtered and cooked animals, one hundred containers of raisins and two hundred of dates. Never would Naval, the selfish husband of Abigail, have organized this kind of gift, not even for the future king of Israel. Risking her life, Abigail follows the donkeys, laden with food, to meet David. In a perfectly phrased speech, using all the powers of persuasion possessed by women, she convinces David to leave the fate of her husband to God, thereby avoiding blood guilt on his hands. With this single act, she clears his path to the Davidic dynasty.[4]

Deborah, Jael, Hannah, and Abigail behave in ways very different from the women in the first Five Books of the Bible. In Genesis, Sarah, Rebecca, Leah, and Rachel seek at critical moments to

---

2. *The Book of Judges*, trans. Rabbi Avrohom Fishelis and Rabbi Samuel Fishelis (New York: The Judaica Press, 1979), 4–5.

3. *The Book of Samuel* 1, trans. Rabbi A. J. Rosenberg (New York: The Judaica Press, 1980), 1:8.

4. *The Book of Samuel*, 1:25.

redirect their husbands, who then take appropriate actions that reflect the wishes of God as they are understood by the women. But the women in Genesis never take over the roles of their husbands.

In the Book of Exodus, the second of the five Books, Miriam advises her father to revoke his decision to separate from his wife, but she takes no action on his behalf. Neither do the wives in Egypt who save the Jewish people by enticing their depressed and hopeless husbands to join them in marital relations and so have children. In the desert, freed from slavery, Jewish women refuse to give their gold jewelry to their husbands who are determined to become involved in the golden-calf episode. But these women do nothing to halt the worship of the calf. They cannot, in fact, stop the men from tearing the jewels from their resisting hands.

Later, the majority of men refuse to cross over to the Holy Land for fear of the giants that were seen there. The women wish to enter Israel, but they do not take any action to obey God's command by crossing over themselves.

The single exception to the women in the *Chumash* is Zipporah, the wife of Moses. She may be foreshadowing and preparing the way for the future. As we have noted above several women in *Tanach* (all the Books of the Bible, which include the Books of Judges and of Kings) have the fortitude, the clarity, and the ability to take drastic action when the men are unwilling or unable to do so.

WHO IS ZIPPORAH?

In Exodus, we learn that the Priest of Midian, Yisro, has seven daughters. They come to the well to draw water for their flocks. On the day that Moses arrives in Midian, the shepherds drive them away. However, Moses, escaping from Egypt where the Pharaoh is determined to kill him, helps the daughters of Yisro, who hurry home to tell their father about the dramatic episode at the well. In response, Yisro asks them to invite Moses "that he may eat bread (marry one of them)."[5] Zipporah, the most beautiful of the daugh-

5. Exodus, *The Pentateuch*, 2:16–20. "Exodus," *Midrash Rabbah*, III, third ed., trans. Rabbi S.M. Lehrman (London: The Soncino Press, 1983), pp. 40ff.

ters, ran after Moses like a bird (*zippor*) and brought him home. By offering the blood of a bird as atonement, "she cleansed the house from every vestige of idolatry."[6] We learn later in the Book of Leviticus, when the laws of purity are given to Moses by God, and then by Moses to the Jewish people, that a ritually impure house had to be cleansed under the jurisdiction of the priest by taking two birds, slaughtering one and using the blood to sprinkle the house seven times, thus cleansing and making atonement for the house "and it shall be clean."[7]

We are not told how Zipporah learned the procedure. Perhaps her house-cleansing, prior to the receiving of the Torah, reveals her innate connection with the Jewish people. It certainly reveals her closeness to God!

In each scene, Zipporah can be seen as understanding hidden truths, taking actions in rapid succession from seeing, to interpreting, to acting. She is daring, creative, alert, fearless, and ready to take on a task, even if it has been delegated to the man in the family, as long as it needs to be done and, for various reasons, the man is not doing it.

Let us attend now to the facts and implications therein.

Prior to the marriage of Moses to Zipporah, Yisro, unsure of the identity of Moses, had him put into prison without food or water. There he remained for ten years. But Zipporah tended to Moses all those years, each day secretly bringing him food and water. Finally, she spoke to her father about "the stranger you placed in prison." Her father assumed that Moses had already died, but again the woman's power of persuasion succeeded. Zipporah said:

> You never know . . . I have heard that the God of the Hebrews has great power and always does miracles. We all know how He saved Abraham from the fiery furnace. There are also many stories about a Hebrew who was placed in the river as an infant, and who was saved by this God. It is told that Pharaoh tried to decapitate him, and the sword merely bounced off his neck. Perhaps this stranger is that

---

6. "Exodus," *Midrash Rabbah*, III, p. 42. On the ritual cleansing, Leviticus, *The Pentateuch*, 14:49ff, pp. 143–144.

7. Leviticus, *The Pentateuch*, 14:52ff, p.144.

very man—he said the Pharaoh had tried to kill him. Where the Hebrew God is involved, nothing is too difficult.[8]

And so Moses and Zipporah are wed. It is possible that their marriage was what is called a Noahide marriage, that is, not a marriage according to Jewish law. Initially, because Yisro and Zipporah had some doubts about Torah concepts, Moses' and Zipporah's Noahide marriage was the type that could be terminated at any time. We shall see shortly how, thanks to Zipporah, their marriage was changed to a traditional Jewish marriage that could be terminated only by divorce.[9]

After the initial marriage, Moses became a shepherd in Midian, settling down with his wife and then his first son. Moses is the model of a kind, thoughtful, very deep person. Everything changes when he encounters the burning bush, and hears the Voice of God calling to him from the bush. In a rapid flow of events, Moses becomes a savior of the Jews who had been enslaved in Egypt for over two hundred years. Although there is much to write about this event, we are attending now to the role of Zipporah. With their two sons, Moses and Zipporah journey to Egypt and, prior to their arrival, spend a night at an inn outside of town. One of the sons, recently born, is in need of circumcision. Commanded by God to go to Egypt, Moses had feared to delay, choosing instead to postpone the mitzvah of circumcision, which would have delayed the trip. It is at the inn that, startlingly, "The Lord met him, and sought to kill him." As the angel of death was swallowing Moses from his head to his membrum (male organ), Zipporah understood at once "the great protective power of circumcision." She understood also that her son should have been circumcised. Remaining clearheaded at this most critical and frightening moment where she faced the possible destruction of her husband and her uncircumcised son, Zipporah takes rapid action. On the spot, with no help whatsoever, she cuts the foreskin from her son. Casting it at the feet of Moses,

8. Exodus I, *Me'Am Lo'Ez, The Torah Anthology,* trans. Rabbi Aryeh Kaplan (New York and Jerusalem: Maznaim Publishing Corporation, 1978), Vol. 4, pp. 66ff.

9. *Chasam Sofer, Commentary on the Torah,* adapted by Rabbi Yosef Stern (Brooklyn, NY: Mesorah Publications, 1996), pp.122, and 128–131.

she says, "Surely a bridegroom of blood are you to me." Later she adds, "You shall be my affianced by a covenant. You are given unto me by merit of this blood of circumcision, because I have fulfilled the command." The angel of death departs, and she says, "A bridegroom of blood in regard of the circumcision." There are a number of explanations of the cryptic and powerful meaning of Zipporah's words. She is acknowledging the power of circumcision, sanctifying the name of God, and predicting the future when Yisro and Zipporah will become full-fledged believers in Torah Judaism so that her marriage to Moses can ascend from the lower level of Noahide marriage to the high level of a traditional Jewish marriage.[10]

After the scene at the inn when the life of Moses is saved, Zipporah and the children return to Midian. The mission of becoming the primary savior of the Jewish people requires that, free of all other commitments, Moses remain in Egypt until the Jews are led out into the desert to receive the Torah at Sinai, and then to continue on to the Holy Land.

When the Jews are liberated, Yisro, Zipporah, and the sons of Moses and Zipporah arrive to meet Moses at Sinai. It is seen as a sign of the righteousness of both father and daughter that they did not abandon Moses. With great patience, a character trait lauded by Torah and seen at its fullest development in Queen Esther centuries later, Zipporah waits until the right time when they learn the ways of the Holy Torah. We see the frightful results of a lack of patience in some of our greatest figures: Adam and Eve, and the sons of Aaron who died worshipping a strange fire. In each case, their decisions and actions were not wrong, but their lack of timing and resistance to seeking direction from God are to blame.

THE ROLE OF ZIPPORAH IS CENTRAL

After all the troubles in Egypt were over, Yisro and his daughter came immediately to Moses. The role of Zipporah is central. The historic meeting is in large part credited to her, for it was Zipporah who found

---

10. "Exodus," *Midrash Rabbah* III, pp. 85, 122.

ways to send messages to her husband to find out exactly where the Israelites would be encamped so that she and her family would know just where to meet him. Moses "had made it plain that he would welcome both Yisro and his family."[11]

Hidden from our eyes, waiting for those seeking to uncover Zipporah's greatness and her message, she models the woman who can, if need be, run after her husband-to-be, save him from death at the risk of disobeying the wishes of her powerful father, a Priest in Midian, take over the role of her husband when he makes an incorrect decision, serves as efficient messenger and organizer for the difficult journey to Sinai. Zipporah redeems through understanding, interpreting, and acting to do the will of God when her father and husband are unable to fulfill some aspect of their missions.

At the same time, Zipporah shows us how a woman can return readily to her feminine nature. There was a time in the desert when Moses could no longer bear the burden of his people, who were challenging his very existence and even his divine mission. As a result, God provided Moses with assistants, seventy elders outstanding for their integrity, wisdom, and leadership. They were given powers of prophecy so they could share some of the responsibilities weighing heavily on Moses alone. As the Israelites were celebrating this occasion, Miriam asked Zipporah, her beloved sister-in-law, what was happening. With joy, Miriam responded to the news, "Happy are the wives of these elders who have merited to see their husbands attain such greatness."[12]

The poignant response of Zipporah—Woe is to these women for their husbands will no longer attend to them—elicited Miriam's question: how did Zipporah know this? Zipporah replied, "Because

---

11. Exodus III, *Me'Am Lo'Ez, The Torah Anthology*, trans. Rabbi Aryeh Kaplan (New York and Jerusalem, Maznaim Publishing Corporation, 1979), Vol. 6, pp. 8ff. "Exodus II," *Or Hachayim*, Rabbi Chayim ben Attar, *Commentary on the Torah*, trans. Eliyahu Munk (Jerusalem, Eliyahu Munk, 1995), Vol. II, p. 627.

12. Numbers, *The Pentateuch*, 4, 11:16ff, pp. 109ff. Numbers I, *Me'Am Lo'Ez, The Torah Anthology*, trans. Rabbi Aryeh Kaplan (New York and Jerusalem: Maznaim Publishing, 1982), Vol. 13, p. 311.

my husband has not attended to me ever since God spoke to him."[13]
We learn that the unique role of Moses required that he be available each time God called him. He had to be ritually pure—that is, free of marital relationship at the time.

Another version tells us that Miriam saw that Zipporah was not beautifying herself as do other women. When asked why she was neglecting her appearance, Zipporah told Miriam that it no longer mattered to Moses whether or not she made herself pretty.[14]

Here we see in Zipporah the essential nature of a woman longing to be cherished by her husband. As always, the Torah tells us that, although taking on a masculine role may be necessary at times, women must return to their true inborn nature. Long after the tale of Zipporah, we find Jael in the Book of Judges protecting her womanliness at the very moment that she is taking on the most aggressive of all masculine roles: slaying the wartime enemy.

WE MAY AT TIMES ACT
IN WAYS UNFAMILIAR TO US

The woman of today may not be placed in the same dramatic position as Zipporah was. Yet life being filled with mysterious, unpredictable happenings, we may at times need to act in ways that are unfamiliar to us. Where does the strength to do this come from? How do we develop and use the skills necessary to perform what can become the small miracles of everyday life? They are there, inside, patiently waiting to be called upon, knowing that, at a moment's notice, we can perform according to the will of God.

Judith was a good wife. With four children ranging in age from 3 to 12 she was "on a forty-eight-hour schedule every twenty-four hours." Her husband, Daniel, was busy as well, involved in real estate. Like many women, Judith had a sweeping knowledge of what his work was all about, but did not understand specific details. Looking at him when he returned from work, she had a sense of whether

---

13. Numbers I , *Me'Am Lo'Ez*, pp. 311–312.
14. Numbers I, *Me'Am Lo'Ez*, p. 312.

his day had been easy or hard. He tried not to burden her, feeling that she had enough to do with the house and the children.

AND THEN IT HAPPENED!

And then it happened. Daniel had a stroke. It attacked the right side of his brain; his left side suffered paralysis. Indistinct words tumbled one upon another, sometimes beyond comprehension. Though the family held out hope that the damage would eventually be reduced, for now, life was in turmoil.

The children seemed to be all right when a part-time helper was brought to care for them. They were able to continue with their routine. But what to do with the business? Phones kept ringing and more demands were placed upon Judith. Although Daniel had a supervisor whom he knew well and trusted, someone had to be in charge of the business. But who? Judith made a decisive move. She would take over the firm. Hiring a full-time caretaker for the children, she plunged into this unknown, strange world of finance, hoping that Daniel would once more resume his position. A sensitive woman, she knew she had to tread lightly so as not to make Daniel feel like an incompetent stroke victim with no abilities. Enhancing his self-esteem during this trauma would be beneficial. Fiercely determined, she set out to explore her new world. First thing first, she grit her teeth and took an intensive crash course on computers.

In a short time, she was able to do all her banking and tracking of properties on-line. With photos on her Web site, she could show her clients the properties before they went to see them. Initially terrified, and feeling that she could never become a computer whiz, she found, to her amazement and delight, that she actually enjoyed it all! Other matters were attended to as well. She spent hours on the phone, ensuring that income came in, bills were paid, and necessary repairs on properties were made. She formed businesslike but gentle relationships with repairmen, electricians, and plumbers. When repairs were necessary, she would call two or three contractors and get estimates before going ahead. And, wonder of wonders, she negotiated and purchased a new piece of property that she thought would be advantageous to the business. On-call and available was that most precious of persons, her computer teacher. Russian born, efficient, brilliant, and caring, this new woman in her life taught her the ins and outs of computer language.

Daniel, she learned, was considered one of the good landlords, a man with a heart, a *guten nashomah* (good soul). Pleased, Judith carried on that tradition. When someone did not pay the rent for several months, because he had been laid off she spoke to him: "I know you're out of work now. I'm truly sorry about that. You've been a good tenant, and I want you to stay. Perhaps you can pay a little of your rent each month. After you get a job, you can catch up. We can work out some payment schedule." The family expressed their gratitude and, over a period of time, the full rent was paid.

JUDITH DID NOT ABANDON HER FEMININE NATURE

With all of this, Judith did not abandon her feminine nature. Not only did she nurture her husband with the necessary physical care he needed, she nurtured his soul as well. "He is still the excellent businessman he was," she said. "I run everything I do past him. When the words are garbled, I untangle them. Somehow, I always know what he means. And when his eyes look up at me, I see the joy and love in them. My heart is full." Even when she knew the answers to questions asked of her, she often took them to Daniel. He was her consult on all decisions, major and minor. The small miracle began to spin into a large one. Daniel moved from wheelchair to a regular chair. Slowly, ever so slowly, his speech became clearer and his left side—hand, leg, and body—became more mobile. After a while, he could walk with a sturdy cane. Some time later, with the help of a driver, he returned to work, a few hours at a time, increasing his hours as improvement continued.

Trauma had created a turnaround in the household. When tragedy strikes, we can get caught in the negative, failing to understand that somewhere in the larger scheme there is a reason for everything. Although it is sometimes indecipherable, in time, God shows us his precious meaning.

Judith and Daniel entered a new relationship in their marriage. She was now not only a partner in their everyday world of home and children, but also a knowledgeable partner and helper in his business. When she was needed, he called on her, sharing decisions and asking her advice. Sometimes he suggested she come in for a few hours to do some computer searching, or talk to tenants and clients who often asked for her "special woman's touch."

When the children were learning to use computers at school, Judith could now help and learn with them. Her bond with them became stronger than ever. Like Zipporah, Judith reached into herself to find inner resources never seen before, becoming a pioneer now as Zipporah was then.

◖❂ 9 ❂◗

Serach: The Wisdom
Of An Old Woman

The first reference to Serach may occur in the Book of Genesis, when Jacob mourns the loss of his son Joseph. "All his sons and daughters arose to comfort him; but he refused to be comforted. . . ." Ramban, an outstanding medieval commentator on the Torah, suggests that the plural form for daughters may include his granddaughter Serach, the daughter of his son Asher. If so, we meet Serach at a time when, like the others in Jacob's family, she fails to console him.[1]

Many years later, the brothers are united with Joseph in Egypt. Fearing that the news that Joseph is still alive may shock their aged father, who could fall seriously ill as a result, the brothers call on Serach. Now an aged woman, known for her sensitivity to music and poetry as well as to people, Serach is successful. She alone can share the good news. She sings a song in which the refrain refers to Joseph as alive:

> Serach took her harp and went to Jacob, singing a very beautiful, haunting melody. She sung that Joseph was alive and a ruler in Egypt; and although she did not sing the words

---

1. Genesis, *The Pentateuch and Rashi's Commentary*, trans. Rabbi Abraham Ben Isaiah and Rabbi Benjamin Sharfman (Brooklyn, NY: S. S. & R. Publishing Company, 1949), 46:17. On Genesis 37:35, see *Ramban, Commentary on the Torah*, trans. Rabbi Charles B. Chavel (New York: Shilo Publishing House, 1971), p. 462.

clearly, Jacob heard them and began to pay attention. Each time he caught the words more and more clearly, and soon he began to understand that she was trying to tell him that Joseph was still alive.[2]

Serach is believed to have lived for almost three hundred years thanks to Jacob's blessing following the exquisite singing that brought him the news that his son Joseph was alive![3]

SERACH IDENTIFIES MOSES

As a very aged woman, Serach reveals the respect with which elderly are held in the Torah. Once the brothers are united, the entire family of Jacob journeys to Egypt and there lives peacefully, respected by the Pharaoh and his people. Once Jacob and his sons die, however, the Jewish people begin to assimilate. Separation between Jew and Egyptian becomes necessary. The enslavement of the Jews eventually results, but here is not the place to detail this phase of Jewish history. What is pertinent is the wisdom of the aged. As a very old woman, Serach is held with such high esteem that she is the one to whom the Jewish slaves will listen, the one they most respect. When Moses is sent by God to bring the Jewish slaves out of Egyptian slavery to become a nation beloved by God, the slaves do not trust him. When Serach hears the words of Moses, "*Pakod pakadeti etkhem*," (I have surely remembered you), she recognizes the secret words of redemption which were transmitted from Abraham to Joseph, from Joseph to Asher, father of Serach, and then to Serach herself. Her identification of Moses as an authentic redeemer is completely respected by the people.[4]

---

2. Genesis, *The Pentateuch*; 45:25–26, "Genesis IV," *MeAm Lo'Ez, The Torah Anthology*, trans. Rabbi Aryeh Kaplan (New York, Jerusalem: Maznaim Publishing, 1977), 3B, p. 463.

3. Genesis, *The Pentateuch*; 45:25–26, "Genesis IV," *MeAm Lo'Ez, The Torah Anthology*, trans. Rabbi Aryeh Kaplan (New York, Jerusalem: Maznaim Publishing, 1977), 3B, p. 463.

4. Exodus, *The Pentateuch*, 3:16; 4:31; "Exodus," *Midrash Rabbah* III, 3rd ed., trans. Rabbi S. M. Lehrman (New York, London: The Soncino Press, 1983), pp. 92ff; 258. "Genesis IV," *Me'Am Lo'Ez*, pp. 97; 125–126.

Moses himself learns the location of the coffin of Joseph from Serach. Joseph had bound the Israelites with an oath to bury his body in the Holy Land, not in Egypt. Weary after searching for three days and three nights, Moses meets Serach in Egypt. She asks, "My lord Moses, why are you tired?" He replies "For three days and three nights I have been going round the city to find Joseph's coffin and I cannot find it." True to the Torah's depiction of women who by nature nurture and care for others, Serach shows Moses where the coffin has been cast into the river by the Egyptians, who wished to keep the Israelites from ever leaving Egypt. Once Serach shows him its location, Moses knows how to draw the coffin forth. Again, a woman's wisdom and a woman's words are effective.[5]

Serach is also identified as the wise woman who saved the city of Abel from destruction. There was a man who had betrayed King David. To protect himself, his son, Sheba, escaped to hide in the city of Abel. David's chief general, Joab, wanted to destroy the entire city in order to assure the death of Sheba. In The Book of Samuel, we learn that there was a wisewoman of the city who knew how to convince Joab to withhold his attack until she could brilliantly convince the inhabitants that they must give up Sheba to Joab. Why this unknown wisewoman is identified with Serach is clear: both are very old, both have a strong association with salvation, and each one knows well "how to arrange her words cleverly."[6]

When Joab and his men were battering the wall of the city of Abel, a "wisewoman called out from within the city":

5. "Deuteronomy," *Midrash Rabbah* VII, 3rd ed., trans. Rev. Rabbi J. Rabbinowitz, pp.178–179. "*Sotah*," *Nashim 3, The Babylonian Talmud*, trans. Rev. Rabbi A. Cohen (London: The Soncino Press, 1978), pp. 67–68.

6. *The Book of Samuel 2*, trans. Rabbi Moshe Ch. Sosevsky (New York: The Judaica Press, 1981), 20:16–19. "Genesis II," *Midrash Rabbah*, p. 877. "Ecclesiastes," *Midrash Rabbah*, VIII, third ed.; trans. Rev. Rabbi A. Cohen, pp. 256, 258. *The Book of Samuel 2*, 14:1–23 and notes pp. 341–349.

"Hear, hear. Say, I pray you" (to Joab): "Come closer . . . so that I may speak to you." And he came near to her, and the woman said, "Are you Joab?" And he said, "I am." And she said to him, "Hear the words of your handmaid." And he said, "I am listening." And she spoke saying, "Surely they should have spoken first [to hear what they have] to say, had they inquired of the people of Abel, and so would they have made peace. I am of those that are peaceful and faithful to Israel. Why then do you seek to destroy a city and a mother in Israel? Why should you swallow up the inheritance of the Lord?"[7]

Joab, agrees that he does not wish to destroy the city but only to be given Sheba, the son of the man who lifted his hand against King David. He replies, "Give us him alone, and I will depart from the city." The woman promises that the head of Sheba will be thrown to Joab over the wall.[8]

In her words to Joab, this wise old woman, Serach, was questioning the renowned scholarship of both Joab and King David. They had failed to follow the procedure outlined in Deuteronomy 20: 10: "When you shall come near a city to wage battle against it, then proclaim peace to it. And it shall be if it makes you an offer of peace and opens to you [you shall not wage battle] but . . . they shall pay tribute to you and serve you."[9]

WOMEN'S WORDS OF WISDOM REDIRECT THE ACTIONS OF MEN OF POWER

Wisdom is clearly associated in the Bible with effective speech. And effective speech is very much a female virtue. Serach may be seen as a forerunner of later depictions of women whose words of wisdom serve to redirect the actions of men of great power: Abigail and Batsheba are examples. Another woman, not of the stature of the

7. "Ecclesiastes," *Midrash Rabbah* VIII, 3rd ed., pp. 256ff; *The Book of Samuel 2*, 14:1–19.

8. *The Book of Samuel 2*, 14:1–19.

9. *The Book of Samuel 2*, 20:17, notes p. 403.

wives of King David, in fact a quite ordinary person, plays a significant role in altering the relationship of David and his son, Absalom. She is known simply as "The Woman of Tekoa."[10]

King David's daughter, Tamar, is raped by her half brother Amnon. As a result, Absalom, another son of David, kills Amnon, revenging the wrong done to Tamar. For this, Absalom is banished by his father. After three years of an exile that created great pain for both father and son, as well as the people Joab, the King's Commander, seeks to reconcile David and his son. To do so, Joab selects a wise woman from Tekoa, directing her to pretend she is a mourner. She is to go to the King and speak to him. "And Joab put the words into her mouth."

Although the text reads, "Joab put the words into her mouth," it is generally agreed that he did not really teach her the parable as such; It is also agreed that only a brilliant woman was capable of presenting the case in a convincing manner, precisely as it had been presented by her; she was expected to improvise replies to David's questions. She is totally successful. David tells Joab to bring Absalom back and Joab prostrates himself and blesses the king.

The case presented by the Woman of Tekoa required great delicacy, adroitness, and modesty. She pretends to be a widow with two sons. One son has killed the other and now the family, anxious for the inheritance, seeks to kill the second son. However, killing him would exterminate her husband's posterity and leave her alone as well. She convinces the king to give the desired ruling and then to confirm it on oath. Only then does she reveal to him that the story is fiction and David's ruling that the murderer will not be punished must apply to his own ruling against Absalom as well.

THE WOMAN OF TEKOA SPEAKS

The story told by the Woman of Tekoa is phrased carefully; it does not clearly parallel the case of David and his son. Thus, the listener does not suspect the connection between the two situations. When she does reveal the truth, her sensitive approach—"If your verdict

---

10. *The Book of Samuel 2*, 20:26; 20:19; "Genesis II," *Midrash Rabbah*, pp. 877ff.

was a sound one for my son, it is equally sound for your son. Therefore do not retract it."—arouses no anger in David at all.[11]

The gift of persuasion is a potential given to women; it may be
used for good or evil. The first woman, Eve, used her persuasive
powers inappropriately. Sarah used the gift effectively, as did
Miriam. And so did others: the Woman of Tekoa and Serach, and
as we shall see, Abigail and Batsheba as well.

That God chose to create the world using words may explain
the morning prayer in which women thank God for creating them
according to His will. It is not unusual to hear women today complain that in the daily prayer, men are thanking God "for not having made me a woman." They interpret this as an indication that
men are feeling superior to women. A more faithful reading would
allow that men may be acknowledging the additional time-bound
mitzvahs they have been given because of their innate limitations
and their willingness to submit to God's will, which has not made
them "according to His will." Rather they must do more than women
to elevate themselves to higher levels. Perhaps one of the most difficult tasks for men is to acknowledge that their spiritual growth
depends largely on the advice women can give them. In this particular prayer, men may be seeking to overcome their resistance to
listening to the words of the wise women in their lives.[12]

WHO ARE THE WISE WOMEN OF TODAY?

Who are our wise women of today? They can be our grandmothers, who are often held in great esteem by their grandchildren, but
are treated in ambivalent and often negative ways by contemporary media.

---

11. *The Book of Samuel 2*, 14:2–23; notes pp. 341–348. See especially
note 13, p. 344.

12. The Morning Blessing: Men say "Blessed are You, God, our God
(God of Mercy), our God (God of Justice), King of the Universe, for not having
made me a woman." Women say, "Blessed are You (God of Mercy), our
God (God of Justice), King of the Universe, for having made me according
to Your will." See the complete ArtScroll Siddur, editor Rabbi Nosson
Scherman (Brooklyn, NY: Mesorah Publications, 1985), pp. 20–21.

When examining novels of high literary merit, researchers found that characterizations of older persons, particularly women, stressed disengagement, voluntary retreat from life, or intergenerational conflict.[13] When older women do appear on television, they are the characters most likely to fail, get hurt, or be killed. It is true, however, that recently, television advertisers and producers have become increasingly aware of the growth of the older population and, consequently its potential as a viable market. They are beginning to present dramas and talk shows, albeit not anywhere near a proportionate number, that depict favorable characteristics in older women.

What are some of the outstanding qualities of older women? A characteristic that has not changed since the time of Serach is "generativity," the desire to make a lasting contribution to the next generation, which manifests itself in the capacity and commitment to care. This desire has a particular developmental course: beginning in early adulthood, it peaks in old age. As women travel from middle age to the later years, there is an increased sense of personal identity and personal effectiveness, along with a heightened sense of exuberance, a joy and excitement about life itself.[14]

WHAT IS WISDOM?

Wisdom is generally associated with old age. But what is wisdom? *Webster's Dictionary* defines wisdom as an "understanding of what is true, right, or lasting," or simply, "good judgment." Psychologists have tried to measure wisdom, but their attempts are still in the infancy stage. Still, psychology agrees that "wisdom is the power to grasp human nature. The wise are comfortable with ambiguity and have expert knowledge in the fundamental pragmatics of life."[15]

---

13. Marcella Bakur Weiner, Jeanne Teresi, and Corrine Streich, *Old People Are a Burden But Not My Parents* (Englewood Cliffs, New Jersey: Prentice Hall Publishing, 1983), pp.166–167.

14. Abigail J. Stewart and Joan Ostrove, "Women's Personality in Middle Age," *American Psychologist*, 53:11 (November, 1998), pp. 185–194.

15. Bertram J. Cohler and Robert M. Galatzer-Levy, "Self, Meaning and Morale Across the Second Half of Life," *New Dimensions in Adult Development*, eds. Robert A. Nemiroff and Calvin A. Colarusso (New York: Basic Books, 1990), pp. 214–263.

As we age, certain changes take place. Prominent among these is the growing awareness, well-developed by the time we reach eighty, of the significance of our lives. We reflect, "What does it all mean? How did I fulfill my dreams? How can I settle accounts with the past?" In this search for meaning over the course of our lives, we become biographers of our own biography. Integrating past and present, we try to make sense of the story of our lives.

GRANDPARENTING

Searching for meaning, we find significance in the roles we play later in life. Grandparenting has vital meaning in the life of the older woman. Different from other relationships, which are often tied to achievement, we are loved as grandmothers for a quality that transcends the visits or the phone calls: just being there. It has been suggested that grandparents are the family watchdogs. Although the grandmother usually waits in the wings, she steps in during a crisis to stabilize the family. She is the family safety net.[16] Grandmothers of today may live in a four-generational family, surpassing the former three-generational ones. It is no longer unusual to find families that include a great-grandmother of ninety or one hundred, a daughter of sixty-five, a granddaughter of forty, and a great-granddaughter of eighteen. The over-eighty-five age group is growing; most live active lives in the community and, contrary to public misinformation, are cognitively intact and physically well. While our mental picture of Grandma may be of a white-haired woman, elderly, disengaged, and near death, grandparenthood today occurs in health and youth. "Old-old-age" is now designated as eighty-five and older. Grandma remains the reservoir of family wisdom and, functioning as the guardian of family history, imparts information about the past.

Grandchildren stay actively involved with their grandmothers. In a national sample of young adult grandchildren, almost 50 percent said that they have weekly contact with their grandmothers,

---

16. Janet Belsky, *The Adult Experience* (St. Paul, MN.: West Publishing Company, 1997), pp. 363–367.

usually the closest of the two grandparents. This grandparent is important to them, the relationship enduring and very close.

Women play a dominant role here. Since grandmothers are more involved with their grandchildren than grandfathers, it is the mother's mother to whom grandchildren report being especially close. Age may be partially responsible, as maternal grandmothers are likely to be younger than paternal grandmothers. The main factor is the daughter. Women control the family's social relationships. Naturally, they want closer contact with their own mothers. The granddaughter is often more attached to her grandmother than her own mother, for she offers protection, unconditional love, and ultimate caring.

Says an adult woman:

> I was raised in Germany and my grandmother lived nearby but not with us. I loved her. Just her being near me made me happy. She also offered protection. My mother was a good woman but had a temper. I remember one day, I must have been about five. I did something my mother didn't like and she went after me with a broom. My grandmother was nearby. She was wearing one of those very long, full skirts. As my mother ran after me with the broom, my grandmother winked at me and lifted her skirts. I ran and hid under them. My mother asked her where I was and, without blinking an eye she said, "I don't know. I haven't seen her!" I was sure my giggling would be heard from under the skirt, but it wasn't. I reluctantly came out from this cocoon a few minutes later when my mother calmed down. She never discovered my hiding place.

Grandmas are the albums of family history, even when suffering from infirmities of aging. One women reports:

> Grandma always lived with us. I adored her. It broke my heart when we had to place her in a nursing home. We made a careful choice. The home had a wonderful reputation but, still, it made me sad. I visited her several times a week, leaving work a little earlier so that I could sit with her in the dining area and watch her eat. I listened to her tales, but also made sure that she was eating well. After the meal, we

would go to her room, before her roommate would return,
so that we could have some time alone. That was the time I
loved the best. I would bring her many family photos. She
would take them out and slowly, but precisely, we would
go over all of them. She would point out all my aunts, uncles,
and relatives whose photos had been taken in the old country. She would give me details of their lives. Her memory
was excellent. How I wished that her body, now physically
so frail and full of ailments, was in better condition. I listened to her stories with the rapt attention I had as a child,
and I put them into my memory. I would hold them there
for safekeeping, to continue the tradition and pass them on
to my own grandchildren and great-grandchildren. That was
my dedicated pledge to myself. My grandma is no longer with
us. God has taken her. But her album of memories lives
inside of me. She will never be forgotten, and I know that
she knows this.

Sometimes a grandma is revered for her exquisite understanding of life, and of people:

Grandma had a candy store. She and grandpa owned it and
worked it together until he passed on. My parents and I
would visit her often since her house was right next to the
store. Before we would go, my mother would give me careful instructions: "Now remember, Grandma has to make a
living from this store. You know Papa and I help her, but
she is very independent and does not like to take from us.
We respect that. So when she offers you something, you can
refuse. We can have it later on, at home." Coming into the
store, my eyes would look hungrily at all the delicacies: a
soda fountain, barrels of different-flavored ice creams, moun-
tains of candy bars. But my favorite was an elaborate ice-
cream mixture. Grandma would ask, "So, Ilene, what would
you like?" Remembering my instructions, I would say,
"Nothing, Grandma. I am really very full." But before these
words had fully left my mouth, the magic had begun: Large
balls of ice cream scooped swiftly onto a long glass dish;
thick chocolate syrup swirled in circles around its center; a
large handful of nuts placed delicately atop each scoop;

a cherry completing this most glorious vision. I would look up helplessly at my mother and shrug defenselessly. What could I do? I had to eat it. I could not offend, now could I?"Grandma knew my innermost wishes and catered to them. She was so wise! And now when people tell me I am smart, I thank Grandma for sharing some of her wisdom with me, for sharing her true understanding of people.

OLDER WOMEN WHO ARE NOT GRANDMOTHERS

What about the older woman who is not a grandmother? It is possible that children who marry later, who choose not to have a family or are unable to, may leave the potential grandmother without grandchildren. But they cannot take her wisdom. Whether or not we are grandmothers in the physical sense, the children in our lives can be our spiritual grandchildren. They seek us out for advice about daily living or female issues, to help plan a bas mitzvah, to provide an understanding of what life was like in "the old days," and to tell stories about our own personal experiences. The grandmother figure is deeply cherished by the young.

Age and its correlate, wisdom, continue to thrive. Statistics are that the centenarian population grew by 160 percent between 1980 and 1990. By 2050, some demographers predict one to four million centenarians. The outstanding characteristics of these survivors, along with their "survivor genes," are their adaptive capacities.[17]

For women through the centuries, the need to nurture, to care, and to offer their wisdom, which they gained as a result of the accumulation of meaningful experience, is as true for us today as it was for Serach in the past. This is the "melody," the song we pass on to our children and they, in turn, pass to theirs. Age is the voice of wisdom.

---

17. Marjorie E. Kettell, "Older Old People," *Journal of Geriatric Psychiatry*," 3:2 (September, 1995), pp. 5–9.

III

Arrivals

✎ 10 ❧

Deborah: Sensitive and Tough

Out of all the nations on earth, I chose a people for Myself, and I thought, so long as the world stands, My glory will rest upon them. I sent Moses unto them, My servant, to teach them goodness and righteousness. But they strayed from My ways. And now I will arouse their enemies against them, to rule over them, and they will cry out, "Because we forsook the ways of our fathers, hath this come over us." Then I will send a woman unto them, and she will shine for them as a light for forty years.[1]

The woman to whom God refers in the above passage is Deborah. Of all the actions for which she is noted, the first to be mentioned is that, as a worthy wife, she spun threads for the temple at Shiloh (the temple built long before the temple in Jerusalem). These threads became the long wicks for candles that her husband would bring to the temple. There they would burn just the exact amount of time needed, different for summer and winter, and her

---

1. *The Book of Judges*, trans. Rabbi Avrohom Fishelis and Rabbi Shmuel Fishelis (New York: The Judaica Press, 1979), Chapters 4–5. Quotation from Louis Ginzberg, *The Legends of the Jews*, (Baltimore: Johns Hopkins University Press, 1998), VI, pp. 34–35, taken from Ps.-Philo, Philonis Judaei Alexandrini *Libri Antiquitatum* (Basil: 1527), 33; 30:1–2.

husband, Barak, would merit life in the world to come, known as *Olam HaBah* (different from the present world, known as *Olam HaZeh*). For this action, God's words are recorded: "Thou takest pains to shed light in My house, and I will let thy light, thy fame, shine abroad in the whole land."[2]

"The whole land" refers to Israel during the period of the Judges, when monarchy for Israel was as yet unknown, and the people had great difficulty following the path hewn by Moses in the desert. As a result, many conquerors ruled Israel. At the time of Deborah the Canaanites ruled under Yaven, King of Canaan, and Sisera, his captain of hosts. Their power was great; they had 900 chariots to wage war as compared to the 600 owned by Egypt at its height of power. For twenty long years, the Jewish people suffered oppression from this mighty foe, and their suffering intensified when the armies of Sisera cursed God constantly.[3]

DEBORAH'S WISDOM
CAME FROM DIVINE INSPIRATION

Married to Barak, a simple man who was head of the Jewish army, Deborah's wisdom came from divine inspiration, making it possible, as we shall see, to effect a drastic change in the position of the Jewish nation as a conquered people. A prophetess, Deborah had the wisdom of a judge. We know that Jewish tradition considers judgeship to be undesirable for women, as it demands total objectivity. A poor woman who steals medicine for her sick child must be judged according to the same law as a wayward teenager who smashes a storefront window to obtain a bottle of liquor. A woman's sensitivity to the plight of others and nurturing powers are important but needed elsewhere.

---

2. *The Book of Judges*, 4:4,: note, p. 28. "*Megillah*," *Mo'ed* 4, *The Babylonian Talmud*, trans. Maurice Simon (London: The Soncino Press, 1978), p. 83.

3. *The Book of Judges*, 4:3. "Ruth," *Midrash Rabbah* VIII, 3rd ed., trans. Rabbi L. Rabinowitz (London, New York: The Soncino Press, 1983), pp.16ff.

"Pesahim," *Mo'ed* 2, *The Babylonian Talmud*, trans. Rabbi H. Freedman (London: The Soncino Press, 1938), p. 610.

In a recent article on the urgent problems faced by Moses in the desert, we learned that Moses calls to God to help him when the nation becomes so difficult that he cannot carry them in his bosom as "a nurse carries a suckling." The Hebrew word for "nurse" is written in the male gender and not in the usual female gender. The explanation given is that a male nurse usually does not tolerate any form of disobedience even from an infant. But a female nurse has the potential to quiet the child, to sing him or her to sleep, to bring about relaxation. When a male nurse is called upon to manage a child properly, he will fail as long as he does nothing to change his natural inclination. Conversely, it is in a woman's nature to nurture and soothe where necessary.[4]

That Deborah is often known to have been a judge in Israel is questioned by others who indicate that her wisdom and gift of prophecy were so great that people came from all over the land to consult with her. Unlike judges who had to travel throughout the country to deliver their judgments, Deborah remained at home, offering her wisdom while seated under a palm tree, in complete view of all who watched her. This is seen as a sign of her modesty. It is not suitable for a woman and a man to be alone together indoors, hidden from view. Modesty is revealed in subtle ways. Ruth, for example, picks up the grain and stalks of wheat left for the poor to gather. To do so, she does not bend, but rather stoops, a modest movement.[5]

DEBORAH, THE GOOD WIFE

Deborah, a woman of wisdom and prophecy, has the qualities of a very good wife as well as of a servant of God, who manifests the

---

4. Numbers, *The Pentateuch and Rashi's Commentary*, trans. Rabbi Abraham Ben Isaiah and Rabbi Benjamin Sharfman (Brooklyn, NY: S. S. & R. Publishing Company, 1949), 11:12. "Ecclesiastes," *Midrash Rabba*, VIII, 3rd ed., p. 98. Rabbi A. Leib Scheinbaum, *Yated Ne'eman* (June 3, 1999), p. 97.

5. "*Megillah*," p. 83, note 3.

quality of modesty even when sought by the great ones of her time. But there is more, much more.

The Jewish people had fallen to such a low level of despair that economically, as well as spiritually, it was as if they had died. The king of Canaan and his army, conquerors for twenty years, had a firm grip on Israel. There was no known way to break that grip— until Deborah stood up and called to her husband (in the midst of prophecy, she could not be with him) to begin the first war since the death of Joshua. (Joshua was the great leader who took over after the death of Moses.) Unfortunately, although he had conquered thirty-one kings in the Holy Land, he had neglected to complete the task; thirty-one more kings lived on, and were enemies of the Jews. It was Deborah who initiated the first war since the death of Joshua, a war that was to succeed. Her words to Barak were clear and strong:

> Hath not the Lord, the God of Israel, commanded, saying, "Go and draw toward Mount Tabor, and take with thee ten thousand men of the children of Naphtali and of the children of Zebulun? And I will draw unto thee to the brook Kishon Sisera, the captain of Jabin's army, with his chariots and his multitude; and I will deliver him into thy hand."[6]

BARAK HAS FAITH IN DEBORAH AS GOD'S INSTRUMENT

Barak responds by agreeing to go against Sisera only if she will go with him. There are several explanations of his response. He may have feared that his 10,000 soldiers would not go against the enemy, or may not have seen himself as worthy of success against such tremendous odds. Clearly the war was not to be won in a natural way. It had to be God's war. This was, after all, the first war since the death of the great leader Joshua. With Deborah behind the offensive, there was hope. Barak had faith in God and in Deborah as God's instrument. She did go, but not without warning her husband that he would lose the credit that comes to one who

---

6. *The Book of Judges*, 4:6, notes pp. 28–29.

initiates the war and the credit for the final victory as well. A prophetess, Deborah knew that another woman, Jael, would kill Sisera—the final victory would come at Jael's hands not her own. Barak is not dismayed, as credit and praise are not what he wants. A simple and good man, he shows great courage. When he stands with his men at the top of Mount Tabor, the safest strategy would be to remain at the top and let Sisera and his men ascend. But when Deborah tells them to leave their position of strength and descend, both Barak and his men follow her direction. They truly believe in the words of the prophetess.[7]

What happens next is all the work of God Who creates a great turmoil in Sisera's camp. Believing that there is a stampede of horses coming toward them, the soldiers break up in a frenzy. Chased by Barak, they fall by the sword. Only Sisera escapes.[8]

JAEL: THE SECOND GREAT WOMAN

And now the second great woman appears. She is Jael. Her husband, a descendant of the family of Yisro, father-in-law of Moses, had lived at one time in the territory of Yaven. Yaven had a treaty with Canaan. Although Jael and her husband now lived in a different area, Sisera assumed that the earlier treaty remained in effect. Thus, Sisera comes to Jael. Alone in her tent, she greeted him with poise: "Turn in, my lord. Turn in to me. Fear not." Covering him with a rug, she soothingly gave him warm milk to drink. "Blessed above woman," Jael then took a tent pin and hammer "and smote the pin into his temples, and it pierced through into the ground; for he was in a deep sleep; so he swooned and died." When Barak later appears, pursuing Sisera, Jael meets him, and says "Come, and I will show thee the man whom thou seekest."[9]

Why did Jael use a tent pin and not a sword? Surely a tent pin is a far more difficult weapon. Have you ever tried to pull one up from the ground? And what strength must be required to hammer it

---

7. *The Book of Judges*, 4:8–9, notes pp. 29–30. 4:14, notes p. 31.

8. *The Book of Judges*, 4:15ff.

9. *The Book of Judges*, 4:17ff.

into the skull of an enemy! It is said that using a sword is taking on the ways of a male warrior. Jael, courageous and strong though she was, knew well that this moment was an exception; she had to do the work of a man. When the moment would pass, she would return to her womanhood and keep developing the potential given to her by God—the potential of every woman to care and nurture those who need help to develop their own strengths as servants of God.[10]

"THE SONG OF DEBORAH,"
ONE OF THE TEN SONGS OF CREATION

The story closes on a very high note: "The Song of Deborah," one of the ten songs of creation. These ten songs are sung only at the highest levels of holiness:

1) Adam when his sin is forgiven (Psalm 92); 2) Moses and the children of Israel at the Sea (Exodus 15:l); 3) The children of Israel when they received the well of water in the merit of Miriam (Numbers 21:17); 4) Moses before he dies (Deut: 32:1); 5) Joshua when he stopped the sun to win a war (10:12); 6) Deborah and Barak (Judges 5:1); 7) Hannah when she gives birth to Samuel (I Samuel 2:1); 8) King David for the miracles that save him (Samuel 22:1); 9) King Solomon, Song of Songs; 10) The song we will sing when redeemed from exile (Isaiah 30:29).[11]

---

10. Rebbetzin Leah Kohn tape "Jael & Yehudith: Women Praised for Manly Pursuits" (Matriarchs Part I), drawn from Midrash on Mishle, 31, YaLikut Shimonei chapter 31. Ramban, "Numbers," Commentary on the Torah, trans. Rabbi Charles B. Chavel (New York: Shilo Publishing House, 1975), p. 285.

11. "Ecclesiastes," *Midrash Rabbah*, p. 98. "*Pesahim*," *Mo'ed* 2, p. 600. "Judges," 5:1, notes pp. 34ff. *Shir haShirim, Song of Songs*, trans. Rabbi Nosson Scherman (Brooklyn, NY: Mesorah Publications, 1977), pp. xxxiv-xlvi. Rabbi A. Sheinman, "*Pesach*: A Trilogy of Shira," *Jewish Observer* (March, 1991), pp. 35–40.

In Jewish tradition, song is not only an instrument for spiritual growth, but also has the powers of atonement, of cleansing of earlier sins, and of preparing the way for the Messiah. It is written that when King Hezekiah was to be appointed messiah, the attribute of justice asked how one who had never sung a song before God could be messiah.[12]

Deborah's song is multifaceted, dealing with the importance of *teshuvah* (regret and confession that signal a return after one has created a gap in the relationship with God), with its widespread effect on the survival of the Jewish people against terrible odds, and with the role of Torah in the unity of all Israel. Deborah knows that the Jews could not have won without God, and she thanks God for letting the nations think they did. She expresses thanks as well for the courage given to the Jews to launch the offensive; even courage is a gift from God.

During the song, sung by Deborah and Barak, there is a moment when Deborah loses her gift of prophecy. Pleading with God to return the inspiration she has just lost, she cries "Awake! Awake!" and inspiration returns. It is said that a drop of arrogance blurred her song when, appearing to boast, she sings, "The rulers ceased in Israel. They ceased until I, Deborah, arose. I arose a mother in Israel."[13]

IT IS NEVER TO LATE FOR REPENTANCE

Haughtiness does not befit women. It is true that every great character in Torah has a flaw, but flaws in great ones are not what they seem. Much is expected of them: The higher one climbs, the more perfect one must be. However, the nature of each flaw can sensitize those who listen carefully. How can the trait of haughtiness block the impact a woman can have? Just as Ruth stooped to gather the grain, so women stoop to keep their eyes level with those who need their encouragement. To lift one's head higher than another

---

12. "*Sanhedrin,*" *Nezikin* 3, *The Babylonian Talmud*, trans. Rabbi I. Epstein (London: The Soncino Press, 1978, p. 630.

13. "*Pesahim,*" *Mo'ed* 2, p. 337. "*Megillah,*" *Mo'ed* 4, p. 85.

is, for that moment, to lose the connection carefully and patiently created. Deborah may have lost that connection with God for a moment, but when she quickly retrieved it by turning to God for help, she reminded us that it is never too late for repentance.

Deborah was the mover and energizer of Barak. Without her encouragement, he was reluctant to face the enemy. She was the tough, determined woman, the decisive one who takes action. But there was another Deborah—the poet who composed and sang songs of thanks to God for delivering the enemy into the hands of Israel's valiant warriors. Unique in her time, she combined marriage with a career, providing a glimpse of what was to come in contemporary society. Deborah was a devoted wife, as well as a prophetess and a judge. People sought her for her words of wisdom. Mutitalented, Deborah could take seemingly opposing characteristics and synthesize them into a glorious whole. As we read her story, we see an adult woman. But seeds for adulthood are planted early. While we know nothing of her early childhood, the path prepared for her by God undoubtedly had help from those around her. What do children need to evolve into a woman like Deborah?

BASIC PERSONALITY TRAITS OF CHILDREN

Children seem to have basic personality characteristics from day one, before they mature through different stages. The absence of straightforward guidelines for the emotional development of the infant and child has created a gap in knowledge, only recently to be addressed. In the past, understanding was focused on parental actions, rather than the baby's feelings or the child's emotional experiences. It is now seen as more of a partnership, child and parent interacting and, more importantly, affecting each other. To understand Deborah's ability to be the kind of woman she came to be, we will suggest some of the milestones she may have passed through.

Born into the world after nine months of peace and quiet, the infant is suddenly barraged with stimuli: sights, sounds, touch, tastes, and smells. To reach out actively to these experiences and, at the same time, remain tranquil is the first rite of passage. The infant can then move on to the second passage, taking a specialized interest in this human world.[14] If pain or discomfort is attached to stage one or two, the infant may not relax; she may not be free to explore this exciting new terrain by smiling back at mother's face, cooing at her, or grabbing a finger held in front of her. With success, stage three can emerge with the infant actively encouraging interaction. Feelings are now at play. She frowns in response to a loud noise or voice, or gurgles with pleasure at something that delights her. Stage four moves in quickly. The baby, close to one year old, connects feelings with behavior, understanding that she has to do something to make it happen. When hungry, she no longer has to sit and cry. Instead, she can take her mother's hand and walk her to the place where food is.

Social, emotional, and behavioral patterns are established. As her world expands, the child recognizes not only her own needs but also the ways of the "giants" surrounding her. Mommy can be sweet or angry or playful or quiet. At the tender age of one and a half, the child becomes aware of her role in their partnership; this seemingly unequal dyad has some equality. And all of this complex orchestration occurs before the age of two. Stage five is a leap. Not only does the child know how things operate but, wonder of wonders, she can use her own mind to create what she needs. If mother is not there the mother's image can be held in the child's mind. The same can be done with a favorite toy not in sight. Stage six is on its way. Now the child can "expand [her] world of ideas into emotional realms of pleasure and dependency, curiosity, assertiveness, anger, self-discipline or setting [her] own limits."[15] Eventually, she learns to separate make-believe from reality, to work with ideas, and to plan ahead. The building blocks have been established. Beginning sensory involvement grows into involvement with others. Interest evolves into love in the form of giving and receiving. Interacting with others, learning to understand them and ourselves, feeling at one with our internal worlds, empathizing with those who need our compassionate understand-

---

14. Stanley Greenspan and Nancy Thorndike Greenspan, *First Feelings* (New York: Viking Penguin, 1985), p. 4.

15. Ibid. p. 6.

ing, forgiving ourselves for our flaws and misdeeds, are all part of the very breaths we breathe as we blossom into adulthood. And so it was with Fran.

FRAN, AN EASY CHILD TO RAISE

Fran was an easy child to raise. Eva, her mother said, "As a new, first-time mother I didn't know what I was in for. But Fran was no problem. When she gave a cry, I would run to soothe her, but by then she would be cooing at the shadows the sun was sculpting on the walls. She seemed to glide through life with the ease and poise of an accomplished dancer. It never ceased to amaze me."

At the age of twenty, Fran married Kenneth, a law student. Helped in part by his parents with their financial aid and with a part-time job, they managed their household well. Despite his busy schedule, Ken was an attentive and caring husband. Fran reciprocated by nurturing him. She typed his law briefs, and helped him prepare for the law exams by feeding him possible questions. She was delighted when he decided to specialize in compensation law: his way, he said, "of helping those who need my help as against just being in it for the money." Life went smoothly. Ken became a lawyer who loved his work. They had a daughter, Jennie.

FRAN: A "PEOPLE PERSON"

When Jennie was in her preteens, her mother decided on a career. A "people person," she wanted to make a contribution to society. She chose social work and was accepted into a good school that allowed her to go part time so that she could continue to be an attentive mother and wife. She earned her degrees with ease. But part of her had a yearning. "I want to help others," she said to Ken, "but I don't think I want to hold someone's hand. Sometimes I think that's what this field is all about." She struggled with her inner turmoil until, one day, a friend spoke about her daughter whom she suspected was on drugs. Fran decided to become a counselor: "I'm going to specialize and get training in becoming a drug and alcoholism counselor." Working for a noted social-service agency, she became a sought-after counselor with a full caseload. She was known to be "tough but fair." Eva, her mother, asked Fran about her work, "What is it like? What does a 'drug addict' look like? how do you talk to them?" Fran described her experiences:

> When someone comes in, I look at their eyes. If their eyes are glassy, if they are very distractible, restless, going from emotional high to low, or laughing one minute and irritable the next, I suspect cocaine, especially if they insist they are not on drugs. My approach is then confrontational, also empathic and sensitive. For example, if their parents are with them, I will not confront their child in front of them. That would be embarrassing and humiliating to my client, and increase the denial as well. I ask parents to leave the room. Then I turn to the young woman or man and say, "If you're not using drugs, then I'm not sitting here in this chair. I'd tell your parents only if I thought your life or someone else's was in danger."

When Eva asked how Fran handled telling the parents, she continued,

> I say, "Why are you afraid to tell your parents? They'll feel better. I'm not going to tell them. You should. But I'll be in the room if that makes it more comfortable for you." And to the parents, I explain that I feel their young-adult child is on drugs, that unless they want to throw her out of the house, this is the way it is going to be. I am direct, "If the two of you want to work out some ground rules for her, and your child is agreeable, you can do that, but it's up to the two of you to decide."

Eva asked Fran, "What happens then?" Fran answered, "The kids usually feel I'm on their side and eventually may give up the drugs. I've had a lot of success with them, and as my colleague, good friend, and former supervisor, Paul says, 'Fran, you're a warm-hearted, tough cookie."

FRAN COMBINES NURTURING
SKILLS WITH CLEAR HEADEDNESS

Fran was successful on the job and in life. Combining nurturing skills with clearheadedness and a straightforward way of being, she danced the "song of life." The seeds planted early in her life and the potential given by God, bore phenomenal blossoms. For women like Deborah and like Fran, we can say, "Many women have done well, but you have excelled them all."[16]

16. Malbim on *Mishley, The Book of Proverbs* in Hebrew and English with the Commentary of Rabbi Meir Liebush Malbim, ed. Rabbi Charles Wengrov (Jerusalem and New York: Feldheim, 1983), 31:29, p. 327.

ᗷ 11 ᗎ

Turning Point: Ruth and Naomi

In the Bible, as in life, there is no suddenness: each event has a beginning. Everything knows a beginning followed by process, occasional returns, and many forward movements. Often the beginnings are dimmed by time and by an absence of awareness in the human mind and memory. But as we study the Biblical stories and the legacy of our women, we can identify beginnings in the Book of Genesis and then follow the patterns that move us toward a glorious future.

Since the coming of the Messiah marks the glorious future, we find its beginning in positive statements that introduce each book of the *Chumash* (the five books that are the foundation and source of everything that follows). Thus, the first book opens with God creating the world. The positive opening—"In the beginning of God's creating the heavens and the earth"—is followed by "when the earth was astonishingly empty, with darkness upon the surface of the deep. . . ." What we discover is that the positive, God's creating, is followed by negative, emptiness and darkness. But very soon, the positive returns. "The Divine Presence hovered upon the surface of the waters," and as we all know, God speaks, "Let there be light," and there is light, and so it goes.[1]

---

1. Genesis, *The Pentateuch and Rashi's Commentary*, trans. Rabbi Ben Isaiah and Rabbi Benjamin Sharfman (Brooklyn, NY: S. S. & R. Publishing Company, 1949), I:1–5.

Next comes the Book of Exodus beginning with the names of the children of Israel who come to Egypt. This is positive, for the seventy original Jewish settlers were "fruitful and increased abundantly and multiplied, and waxed exceedingly mighty; and the land was filled with them." We could say from ascent, there is descent and then ascent, higher and greater than the period before the descent. A pattern emerges and continues throughout the books of the Bible as well as throughout the history of the Jewish people.[2]

Well may we ask now: how does the *Book of Ruth* relate to this pattern of creation, destruction, and greater creation? Ruth's spiritual antecedent is Tamar. In the Book of Genesis, Tamar knows through divine insight that she must wed a member of the family of Judah. Ready to sacrifice her life if need be, she serves as God's emissary to prepare the way for the Messiah. Because of her saintly decisions and actions, her efforts are fruitful. She becomes the mother of the ancestor of King David, Perez (ancestor of Boaz who marries Ruth who bears Obed, the grandfather of David in whose line the Messiah will be born).[3]

In the *Book of Ruth*, the pattern of Creation from descent to greater ascent is found in the story itself and, in particular, in the life of Ruth, its heroine. Chapter One opens with a famine in Bethlehem, Israel and, more terrible, information that the outstanding family of Elimelech including his wife, Naomi, and their two sons, Mahlon and Chillion, is leaving the Holy Land and settling in enemy territory, Moab, a spiritually barren land, antithetical to the values implanted in the Jewish people at Sinai. The story opens in descent and continues thus until a moment of light shines with Ruth, the Moabite wife of one of Naomi's sons, insisting that, despite great hardship, she will join Naomi to journey to the Holy Land. "Your people are my people, and your God is my God."[4]

The background: When Elimelech, husband of Naomi, left the Holy Land and settled in Moab, where they lived for about ten years,

---

2. Exodus, *The Pentateuch*, I:1–7.

3. On Tamar, see Chapter 5 of this book.

4. *The Book of Ruth*, 2nd ed.; trans. Rabbi Meir Zlotowitz (Brooklyn, NY: Mesorah Publications Ltd., 1976), I:16. Dr. Blema Feinstein, "Saga of the Princess Disciple," *Bas Ayin*, Issue Eleven (Great Neck, NY: December, 1976), pp. 40ff.

his wife, Naomi, understood that this was not right. Unlike other wives in the Bible, she could not convince her husband to remain in Bethlehem, but decided to join him nevertheless. Here we have an example of the woman who knows what is right, yet does what is wrong because she chooses to remain with her husband. As a result, Naomi's suffering was great—"I was full when I went away, but God has brought me back empty." For after they left the Holy Land, Elimelech died, and their two sons married foreign princesses of Moab, named Orpah and Ruth. Later the sons died. Naomi was bereft and poverty-stricken. But what could have become a valley of hopelessness and despair rose slowly toward heavenly heights. Naomi decided that poor though she was, she could return to the Holy Land. Surely, she knew that the residents of her homeland would be shocked to see her present condition. After all, she had been the richest woman in town and the most pious as well. Nevertheless the good woman returns to her roots.[5]

A LIGHT SHINES IN THE DARKNESS

Ruth and Orpah were Moabite princesses who married Naomi's two sons. When Naomi decided to return home, she sought to dissuade her daughters-in-law from joining her. Orpah returned to her rich beginnings (to sink thereafter to the lowest levels of depravity), but Ruth refused to return to her ancestral place. She was a convert, dedicated, firm, clear, and so much a model of the Jewish woman who should and can be, that we read her story on the holy day of Shavuos, the day that recalls the receiving of the Torah at Sinai. We must look now more closely at Ruth.[6]

When Ruth and Naomi arrive in Bethlehem, the women are shocked to see the condition of Naomi: "Could this be Naomi?" Her reply is, "Do not call me Naomi [pleasant one]. . . . Call me Mara [embittered one] for the Almighty has dealt very bitterly with me."[7]

---

5. *The Book of Ruth*, I: 19–22.

6. *The Book of Ruth*, I: 16–18.

7. *The Book of Ruth*, I: 20. "Ruth," *Midrash Rabbah*, VIII, 3rd ed. trans. Rabbi L. Rabinowitz (London and New York: The Soncino Press, 1983), pp. 47–48.

Now the light will shine more steadily. We are given the first hint of the special qualities of Ruth when her mother-in-law seeks to persuade both her and her half sister, Orpah, to return to their home, the palace where they had lived before they married the sons of Naomi. Naomi is very clear about the disadvantages of remaining with her: she is poor, and too old to remarry and have sons who could marry them. They would be going to a strange land where in all likelihood they would be shunned since the Moabites had a history of hating the Jewish people. To become converts, they would have to abide by religious restrictions that were far removed from the lives they had been used to. Nevertheless, Ruth's response is unadulterated. In her purity, she is clear, devoted, and determined:

> Do not urge me to leave you, to turn back from following you. For where you go, I will go. Where you lodge, I will lodge. Your people are my people, and your God is my God. Where you die, I will die, and there I will be buried. Thus may God do to me, and so may He do more, if anything but death separates me from you.[8]

It is said that Ruth converted at this point, for the text reads that when Naomi saw that Ruth was determined to go with her, she stopped arguing "and the two of them went on until they came to Bethlehem." "The two of them" went together, suggesting that Ruth is now a convert. Others believe that the conversion occurs after they arrive, three months later.[9]

A subtle hint of the inner strength of Ruth appears when Naomi explains to the residents of her town that she is bereft, that "God has brought me back empty." Ruth, her loyal, precious daughter-in-law is standing at her side. Most of us would be feeling slighted, saddened, and rejected if our dearest mentor were to talk about being empty, while we stood by her side. Not Ruth—her inner strength and commitment are strong enough to hold her tall and dignified regardless of external blows. Naomi does not intends to

---

8. *The Book of Ruth*, I:16–17.

9. *The Book of Ruth*, I:19. "Ruth," *Midrash Rabbah*, p. 47, note 7.

offend Ruth; Naomi is acknowledging her suffering, which may be intensified by her guilt at leaving the Holy Land and remaining in Moab for so many years.[10]

WHEN A WIFE CANNOT BUILD
THE SPIRITUALITY OF HER HUSBAND

The close relationship between Naomi and Ruth goes deeper than surface appearances. Remembering that Naomi was unable to influence her husband to do the right thing, namely, to remain in the Holy Land regardless of the famine, we discover that even so redemption is possible. If a wife cannot build the spirituality of her husband, she can turn her attention to others who are near. Ruth chose to follow Naomi, who was not only her mother-in-law but her mentor as well. Naomi is the teacher and guide of Ruth, and she takes her mission very seriously, as we shall see.[11]

The two women are penniless, but there is property in Naomi's family. Were Ruth to marry a relative of her departed husband, that property would be the dowry; according to Jewish law, the name of the departed husband would be redeemed. Mystically speaking, a child born to the couple in the second marriage could be the reincarnation of the departed husband who now has a second chance to live a life holier than the one he has left. Naomi plays a significant role in moving Ruth toward Boaz, whom she will marry.

Before this marriage can take place, a series of events must prepare for it. When the two women reach their destination, they have to find a way to survive. Too proud to ask for help, Naomi bears the guilt of her departure at a time of famine when her family could have helped those less rich. With understanding, Ruth offers to find a field in which to glean ears of grain (a Jewish law requires landowners to leave ears of grain behind for the poor).

---

10. *The Book of Ruth*, I: 21.

11. Rebbetzin Tzipporah Heller, "Woman's Relationship with Herself, with God & with Others," The Second International Jewish Women's Conference (New York City: May 2, 1999).

12. *The Book of Ruth*, II: 2ff; notes pp. 86–88.

She is praised for offering to glean like a common pauper "to spare her mother-in-law the indignity of going out and being subject to the humiliating gazes of those who knew her in her former affluence."[12]

RUTH CHOOSES TO STOOP, A SIGN OF HUMILITY

When most would bend over to pick up the fallen grains, Ruth chooses to stoop. It is clear that bending over is less modest than stooping, but there may be a more hidden meaning. To stoop is to maintain eye level with one who may be less developed, either physically or spiritually. To bend is more condescending. To emulate Ruth is to develop one's kindness, loyalty, modesty, humility as well as the commitment to wholeheartedly serve God.[13]

The owner of the field, Boaz, a man in his eighties who has just lost his wife, judge and leader of his community, is a man of great distinction and character. As soon as he sees Ruth gleaning in his field, he knows she is special and inquires about her from his overseer. Following this, we find Boaz engaging Ruth in conversation, offering her wise advice and words of comfort and praise. Ruth responds with warmth and gratitude, but one of her replies, translated in different ways, may be controversial. After she has asked to continue to find favor in his eyes, she adds words literally translated as, "And I will not be as one of your maid-servants." Interpretations vary: "Though I am not as worthy as one of your maidservants" or "I am not even worthy enough to be as one of your maidservants." The one that seems to us to reflect a Ruth of dignity and commitment is, "I am not like one of your maidservants who perform good deeds for the sake of reward. My intentions are only for the sake of heaven." Here we see the strength and courage at the core of Ruth.[14]

---

13. Rebbetzin Tzipporah Heller, "The Light of Awareness," *Hamodia* (May 21, 1999), p.75. "Shabbath," *MO'ED I, The Babylonian Talmud*, trans. Rabbi Dr. H. Freedman (London: The Soncino Press, 1978), p. 555.

14. "Ruth," *Midrash Rabbah*, pp. 50, 81. *The Book of Ruth*, II:13. Dr. Blema Feinstein, p. 41, p. 43, note 2.

NAOMI BRINGS MATTERS TO A CLIMAX

During the three months of harvesting, Naomi has been guiding Ruth, preparing her well. Knowing that Boaz is a relative of her husband and well equipped to become the husband of Ruth, which would open the door of redemption for her deceased son, Naomi brings matters to a climax: "Bathe and anoint yourself, don your finery, and go down to the threshing floor, but do not make yourself known to the man until he has finished eating and drinking. And when he lies down, note the place where he lies and go over, uncover his feet, and lie down. He will tell you what you are to do." With reluctance, Ruth agrees: "All that you say to me I will do." But, understanding that it is not appropriate to walk through town in her Sabbath finery, Ruth waits until she arrives at the threshing floor. All goes well. Boaz agrees to marry Ruth and so perpetuate the name of the deceased, but first he must make the offer to a nearer relative who may agree to be the redeemer, but, the next morning, declines the offer. Boaz, and not the nearer relative, marries Ruth. A son is born (after the death of Boaz). His name is Oved, grandfather of King David.[15]

Surprisingly, "Naomi took the child and held it in her bosom, and she became his nurse." The women say to Naomi, "Your daughter-in-law [Ruth], who loves you, has borne him, and she is better to you than seven sons." This sentence stands in remarkable contrast to the one in the book of *Samuel*. There we find Elkhana trying unsuccessfully to cheer Hannah, who is barren for eighteen years. He asks her, "Am I not better to you than ten children?" Can we say that when husband or sons cannot or will not grow spiritually, the wife and mother can impact successfully on others? God sends us those whom we can nurture: if not husbands, if not children, then children of others may await our care. [16]

---

15. *The Book of Ruth*, III:3–5; IV:13. "Sanhedrin," *Nezikin* 3, *The Babylonian Talmud*, trans. Jacob Shachter (London: The Soncino Press, 1978), pp. 99–104. *The Zohar*, II, trans. Harry Sperling and Maurice Simon (London and Jerusalem and New York: The Soncino Press, 1934), p. 218.

16. *The Book of Ruth*, IV:15–17. On Hannah, see Chapter 13 of this book.

TRULY COMPASSIONATE GIVING

Contemporary society emphasizes the need to be loved. "Find some-one who will cherish you, give to you, understand you" are domi-nant themes with the implicit warning that unless you are given to, life is empty. Left out of this equation is the need to give. Through giving to others, we fulfill ourselves. This form of giving reflects neither self-satisfaction, egoism, or the craving for credit and praise. Truly compassionate giving, strange to say, leads to inner satisfac-tion far greater than ego-directed kindness.

In today's world Naomi and Ruth would be seen as the true "odd couple." Daughters-in-law and mothers-in-law are depicted as an-tagonists, with husband sandwiched between, trying to placate both wife and mother. Mothers-in-law are seen as particularly ominous, holding on to their sons at any age and viewing their wives as "the other woman." Yet, folk myths to the contrary, the truth is of an-other nature.

Becky and Morris had been married for over a quarter of a cen-tury. Now in their mid-fifties, with two young-adult children, life was good and they were grateful. No major illnesses or problems, children who honored their parents, respected tradition, and owned enough worldly goods to enable them to be charitable. But Becky and Morris did suffer losses in the deaths of Becky's parents from cancer, both within two years and, for Morris, in the death of his father in a car accident. The only parent still alive was Nina, Morris's mother.

NINA LIVED AN INDEPENDENT LIFE

Nina had always lived an independent life. Strong and energetic, she had many interests. Active in her community, she also had a hobby that in her later years, turned into a business. She designed and made clothes for herself and her clientele. Many a woman wore her outfits with pride, for Nina put her heart and soul into her work.

But of late, there had been some changes. They seemed to come slowly but insidiously. Becky and Morris noticed them. "I don't know what's happening with my mother," said Morris. "She seems to be forgetting so much. In all these years, she has never forgotten my birthday, and this time she did. When I told her that it was my birthday, she frightened me by saying, 'Who is this?' I tell you, Becky, that really scared me." Becky said, "Well, let's see how it goes. Perhaps she is overloaded with work. Besides, you and I, only in our fifties, also sometimes forget. How many times do we walk into a room knowing that we were coming in for something and then just stand there wondering what it was we came for? And how many times do we forget what to shop for without our list?" Morris was reassured. But not for long. Nina, always so tastefully dressed, so scrupulously clean about herself and the house, was becoming neglectful. Her dresses were wrinkled, her hair was in disarray, and dishes piled high in the sink.

They decided to check on her more often. Either Morris or Becky visited several times a day. One day they visited but Nina was not at home. On this cold, blustery day, they wondered where she had gone. They had talked to her only a short time earlier, preparing for their visit. Morris was frantic: "Stay here, Becky, in case she returns. I'm going to tour the area and see if I can find her." He found her a short while later. She was in a public phone booth, a notepad in her hand, tears running down her cheeks. "Mama, Mama, what are you doing?" asked Morris. Nina hesitated. Her words came slowly, as though she were searching the air to find the right ones: "I don't know. Where am I? I was going for a walk but could not find my way back. Am I near my house, or yours? I don't know. I don't know. Will you take me home?" "Of course, Mama. Don't worry. Take my arm. We will be home in a few minutes." He took Nina's arm and put it under his, holding tight. He was devastated, fighting back his own tears. Becky, relieved to see the two, noticed that Nina had gone out without her winter coat. She said, "Mama, it's cold out-side. Would you like a nice, warm bath? I'll help you into the tub. Is that OK with you?" Grateful, Nina nodded. Becky turned to Morris: "Honey we have to do something. This cannot go on. We'll be sitting at the phone all day and worrying day and night. We have to make some changes. The last time she had some tests, they found nothing wrong except that her blood pressure was a little high, but not dangerously so. But I spoke to my friend Anna who has worked with older people as a social worker. She told me that, according to all that is known, there may not be any relationship between the person's behavior and what tests show. Science has only gone so far and no further. So it's up to us to come up with a solution." Morris agreed, "I hate to think it but what about a nursing home? I remember when my Uncle Sam was in one. He was well taken care of. It may be the best thing for everyone."

SHE IS NO LONGER THE MOTHER I HAD

Becky looked at him for a long time without speaking. "No. Absolutely not," she said. "Never, while I am alive. And, frankly, honey, I am surprised you even mentioned this." "Well," said Morris, "it's just that I don't know what to do. I feel so bad. Seeing her this way. . . . It just destroys me. She's no longer the mother I had. I'm losing her, day by day." Becky went over and kissed him. She replied, "I know. I'm not blaming you. Truly I'm not. But we can do something that will help. Your mother can come to live with us. I'm home much of the time, and when I'm not, our daughters can help out. When they cannot, we'll get someone in for a few hours. There are many people around, and I'll ask Anna to get us someone good. I'll supervise to make sure all goes well. At least she'll be right here, under our very noses. Nursing homes may be good for some people, but if there is family, why assign someone like your mother a life away from home, surrounded by strangers, even well-meaning ones? Perhaps if she were very ill and needed total nursing care, I would consider it. But she doesn't." Becky moved closer to Morris and held his face in her hands, continuing, "Besides, darling, I love her. I love her for who she is—this strong, beautiful woman who gives so much of herself to others for all the years I have known her. And who gave me you. How could I abandon her?" Morris didn't answer. He just put his cheek against Becky's face and whispered in her ear, "You're an angel. How blessed I am to have you."

NINA'S LIFE TAKES A TURN

Nina came to live with her son, daughter-in-law, and granddaughters. The room that had been a study for Morris and Becky was turned into a bedroom. A bathroom was constructed, joined to the room for her private use. Techniques were used to help her with her memory. Little stick-on notepads were placed around the house as a form of wall decoration. Colorful and large, they said things like, "Mama, it is now 2:00 P.M. Morris and I will be back in two hours, at 4:00 P.M." On the refrigerator door, in bold letters, "Mama, your lunch is on the bottom shelf, wrapped in wax paper. It has your name on it. Enjoy. Be back real soon. Love." Nina's sewing machine was placed in a corner of her room with patterns and the things she would need for her work neatly displayed. All was labeled. At night, when everyone was home, Nina would join them, when she wished, in any activity they were engaged in. When friends visited, sometimes she came in for a short while and then retired. She was appropriately dressed and cared for. Outside help was informed of Nina's special likes and dislikes, and close attention was paid to the care she was receiving. Fortunately, Becky and Morris did not have the problems adult children sometimes have when a parent comes to live with them. This often revolves around aggressive behavior: scratching, kicking, biting, hitting, and verbally assaulting caregivers and family. Accompanying this may be paranoid ideation such as, "You are trying to put me away. I know that. You can't fool me," or "You are poisoning my food." But Nina's pleasant, appealing disposition did not change. She appeared grateful for all that was done for her.

While Nina's memory did not improve, it was not treated as an unhealed wound. Rather, it was accepted for what it was: short-term and some long-term memory loss leading to confusion and disorientation in place, person, and time, attributed to a form of Alzheimer's Disease or depression or, more likely, a combination of the two, since they are often indistinguishable.

Nina, living at home with her children, energized by their pure, devoted, and selfless love, lived the rest of her life in a blessed, protective setting. And she was not the only one to benefit. For, in her giving, Becky, the daughter-in-law par excellence, like Ruth, learned what it meant to give. In so doing, she also received. And God never forgets.

❧ 12 ❧

Manoah's Wife:
A Remarkable Woman

"If the Lord wanted to kill us . . . he would not have shown us all these things." To help calm his students at a crucial moment during the Holocaust, Rabbi Wasserman quoted this verse. They are words from a passage in the Bible, spoken by the woman who became the "mother of Samson." Not widely known, Hatzlalfonee is the wife of Menoah, described as a woman of deep religious spirit. She is certainly worthy to be the mother of a deliverer of Israel. Samson was intended to become the Messiah, but a single significant flaw made this impossible, as we shall see. Never in the Bible is there so much attention given to the birth of an important person. There are hints in the Book of Genesis when Abraham and then Sarah are informed of the birth of Isaac to take place in the following year, but this announcement is all that takes place. In the case of the birth of Samson, we read in detail about the announcement:

AN ANGEL APPEARED TO THE WOMAN

"And an angel of the Lord appeared to the woman, and said to her, "Behold now, you are barren, and have not borne; and you shall conceive and bear a son. Consequently, beware now, and do not drink wine or strong drink, and do not eat any unclean thing. Because you shall conceive, and bear a son; and a razor shall not come upon his head, for a

Nazirite to God shall the lad be from the womb; and he will begin to save Israel from the hand of the Philistines."

Samson was unique. Unlike Samson, a nazir is rarely one from birth. He may take the pledge to abstain from wine, from grapes, from cutting his hair, or from touching a dead body for a limited period of time, because he has discovered that he cannot control his drinking. To be born a nazir is Samson's unique gift and mission. His mother had the merit to prepare herself and her baby to serve God totally. Descending from the tribe of Judah, the ancestor of the Messiah, Hatzlalfonee was a remarkable woman.[1]

Unlike the message delivered by an angel to Abraham and then to Sarah, the message in this *Book of Judges* appears first to the wife and only then to Menoah, her husband. In fact, we are led to believe that the message was not originally intended to be given to the husband at all. Here, every detail is carefully spelled out to the wife. When she returns to tell her husband about the encounter, she changes some of the words: "A man of God came to me, and his appearance was like the appearance of an angel of God, very awesome. . . ." Because Manoah pleads with God to let this "awesome man" come again and teach them what to do "to the lad that will be born," God hears his words. The angel of God appears again to the woman who was sitting in the field. Again her husband was not with her.[2]

THE RIGHTEOUS ALWAYS HASTEN ENTHUSIASTICALLY

Hatzlalfonee now hurries and runs to tell her husband that this wondrous man has appeared to her again. We read "hurried" and "ran" and come to realize that the Torah is revealing something glorious about this woman, that "The righteous always hasten enthusiastically."[3] Further, this is a wife eager to please her husband,

---

1. *The Book of Judges*, trans. Rabbi Avrohom Fishelis and Rabbi Shmuel Fishelis (New York: The Judaica Press, 1979), 13:23. The story is told in Chapters 13–16. All quotations are from this edition.

2. *The Book of Judges*, 13:3–6; note p.109.

3. *The Book of Judges*, 13:8–9.

to lead and direct him in warm and considerate ways. She reminds us of Deborah, who also sought to increase the merit of a husband not quite at her level of spiritual development. Manoah descended from the lesser tribe of Dan, and his wife from the great tribe of Judah. She did not wish to embarrass her husband by telling him all the details she had learned about the child to be born and his destiny. Rather she spoke about things that related only to her conduct during the pregnancy. Not until the angel speaks to him does Manoah hear that his wife had already been informed about everything that pertained to her and to the child as well. She knew how to speak and how to refrain from speaking, an asset to many marriages, particularly where it is likely that the husband will otherwise sense his inferiority in certain areas.[4]

Equally astounding is the ability of Hatzlalfonee to control herself in the face of a situation that must have overwhelmed her. This type of restraint is found also in Abigail and later in Esther. Women have nine powers of speech and, when appropriate, powers of restraining speech as well. Manoah's wife held back much more than words about the encounter with the angel. This proved her merit and preparedness to be spoken to by an angel. Realizing that the Philistines would seek at once to kill a person with the strength to fight all the wars alone—a unique power and method of battle—she did not let it be known that Samson would be fighting all alone.[5]

That Manoah was not on the level of Abraham is further shown when, wishing to show gratitude for the child to come, Manoah asks for the name of this messenger. In contrast, Abraham was quick to show honor to his guests without knowing who they were and without asking for their names. Neither Abraham nor Manoah knew at first that their visitors were angels.[6]

Finally, when they offer a sacrifice to God and the angel ascends in the flame, Manoah and his wife come to realize that they had

---

4. *The Book of Judges*, 13:10, note 10, p.111. "Numbers 1," *Midrash Rabbah* V, 3rd ed., trans. Judah J. Slotki (London and New York: The Soncino Press, 1983), pp. 361–363.

5. *The Book of Judges*, 13:7, note 7, p.110c.

6. *The Book of Judges* 13:17, note p.113.

been visited by an angel. Their response differs markedly. Manoah says, "We shall surely die, because we have seen God." His wife replies, "If the Lord wanted to kill us, He would not have received from our hand a burnt offering and a meal offering, and He would not have shown us all these things; and at this time He would not let us hear such things as these."[7]

THE WOMAN CALLED HIS NAME SAMSON

The very next verse tells us that "the woman bore a son and called his name Samson." The name selected by his mother, Samson—in Hebrew, Shimshon—includes the name Shamash, servant of God; Shimamah, destruction that would come to the Philistines, enemies of the Israelites, through her son; and Shemesh, the Sun. Clearly she was a woman of great imagination, intelligence, and sensitivity.[8]

The tragedy of Samson is well-known. Beginning in holiness, Samson was prepared for the role of savior even before his birth. He was successful in every undertaking, his physical strength an expression of inner strength and power. However Samson's greatest test was his assurance that he would be the savior of his people. By assurance we do not mean ego or arrogance, rather a holy trust in God and readiness to do all in his power to bring about the redemption. Samson was like many great men before him, including Adam; the sons of Aaron; Korach, and the two hundred and fifty men who joined his rebellion against Moses and thus against God; and the Israelites who worshipped the golden calf, having journeyed from Sinai confident that they would do God's will without further help from Him. Samson's weakness was in his strength; he forgot to continuously call on God for help. Without this help, no human could have the strength to ignore the manipulations of a woman like Delilah. As preparation for the role of Messiah, Samson un-

7. *The Book of Judges*, 13:33–23.

8. *The Book of Judges*, 13:24, note 24, p.114. "*Sotah*," *Nashim 3, The Babylonian Talmud*, trans. Rev. A. Cohen (London: The Soncino Press, 1978), pp. 43ff.

derstood that it would be necessary to have a worthy mate, a remarkable woman who would serve as true *ezer kenegdo* (helpmate). That "he loved a woman by the brook of Sorek, and her name was Delilah," recalls the reference to Jacob and Rachel—"Jacob loved Rachel" when he saw her at a well. But like Eve, and unlike Rachel, Delilah falls to the blandishments of her Philistine lords. They rewarded her well for persuading Samson to reveal the secret of his mighty strength and power. Actually, Delilah's attempts lasted over a period of time. Initially, Samson responded negatively to her urgent questioning; she would ask, "Tell me now, wherein is your strength so great, and with what you may be tied up to torture you" and "Behold you have mocked me, and told me lies. Immediately, now tell me, with what you may be tied up". But that Samson responded at all was a sign of weakness. Somehow, he was beginning to lose faith. It was as if realizing that Delilah was not the wife intended for a messiah, he began to lose hope. Instead of turning to God for help and direction, he was beginning to lose hope as was true of other men in the Torah (the father of Moses, the Jewish slaves in Egypt, the men who worshipped the golden calf fearing that Moses would never return, the spies and the men who refused to enter the Holy Land, Hannah's husband, and Samson's father). In the case of the others, women stood by, often succeeding in turning the tide from despair to hope and renewal. But like Adam, Samson did not have the helpmate that he needed. He became a failed messiah, and finally giving in to the persuasion of his wife, he revealed the secret. When his hair was cut off by his enemies, he lost his strength. Where the words of Sarah, Miriam, Abigail, Huldah, and others brought salvation, the words of Eve and Delilah brought destruction.[9]

If words can bring destruction, they can also be used to unleash creative energy and add goodness to the world. Sometimes it takes a seemingly ordinary woman to do this, although, in truth, such a woman is far from ordinary.

---

9. *The Book of Judges*, 16:4–13. Rebbetzin Leah Kohn, "Delila: A Missed Opportunity," Matriarchs, Part 1, tape sets prepared by The Jewish Renaissance Center, available through Zalman Umlas, (718) 252–5274, drawn from *Bereshis* Rabbah 98:14.

NELLIE AND FRED ARE TIGHTLY BONDED

Nellie and Fred were very different from each other, but they had developed the art of compromise in their marriage. Fred was very neat and exacting in his ways; Nellie was looser and, by her own admission, sometimes lax and careless in her style. Yet, married now for six years, they were tightly bonded. During off season, when his accounting skills were in less demand, Fred sought to spend more time with his wife and Nellie spent more time with Fred when she was not working as a teacher with preschool children. They had similar likes in food, friends, and devotion to their tradition. But one difference created problems of a gigantic nature: Fred's stinginess. While they were still young and hoping for a family, his miserliness seemed to be increasing year by year. Nellie noted the signs early on but attributed it to situational stresses: first a beginning marriage, and monies to buy a modest little house with furnishings; then monies peeled off for savings to prepare for Fred's seasonal business with its frantic demands followed by a lull, and now Nellie's job dangling on a thread due to the school's financial problems. She also intended to cease full-time work once she became pregnant, something both deeply longed for.

There was no need, however, for tightness of money. They had saved a good amount; and their income was enough to afford them all the necessities and many luxuries. Both were young and healthy with bright futures ahead. Still, each time they went over their finances, Nellie would point out the reality of their situation compared to Fred's anxiety, and seemed to get nowhere. A bright man in a constant state of tension and anxiety, Fred would always comment, "What if?" "What if one of us is no longer able to work? What if suddenly no one needs accountants? What if you cannot work even part time?" Patiently, time after time, she reiterated her litany of how all of these worries were needless. But what disturbed her most of all was his increasing inability to be charitable. Now an integral part of their community, Nellie wished to share their resources with others. She knew and wished to adhere to the law that a percentage of their income should go to charitable causes of their choosing. Fred, generally kind in his giving time to others, was adamant in these instances. "We can't give this year," he would say to Nellie. "I don't want to be in the position of having to go to others for help. Nor do I want to ask my parents or yours or even our rich uncle. I would be ashamed. We'll just have to say 'No,' Nellie. Some other time, maybe, but not now."

NELLIE LIVED A SECRET LIFE

Nellie was distraught and, contrary to her views about marriage and feelings about Fred, she started to put aside monies on her own. She told Fred nothing about this and asked whomever she gave the money to, not to divulge the giver. But she felt pangs of guilt. She was living a secret life, involved in an affair-of-the-heart without her husband's knowledge. Even so, she kept up her separate life as things plummeted from bad to worse. When they had guests for dinner, Nellie, priding herself on her cooking, would be preparing the food in the kitchen. Fred would come close and watching her preparations, say, "Nellie, are you giving all of this away? What will be left for us? Will we have some food for tomorrow? Save us something."

When Nellie would be putting together some clothes for a clothing drive to take place at her school, her husband would ply her with questions—"Nellie, why are you giving that away? You could still use that. I could find some use for this, for that, for all these things." She saw the look of fear in his eyes. It was a look of desperation as if each time he gave something away, he lost a piece of himself. He acted as if he had only so much to give, a fixed quantity, no more, no less. Each stripping away from that mass meant he was destitute, impoverished, and in despair. An intelligent, educated woman, she recognized that this was different from hoarding. For hoarders, and she had known some, took pleasure in their accumulations. As in children's fairy tales, misers pored over their monies, fanatic glee in their eyes with every counting. Collectors of art, antiques, or prized possessions also revelled in this treasure chest as they squirreled away more and more.

But Fred did neither. He was just relieved knowing that nothing of theirs had been given away. It reminded Nellie of her 2-year-olds who, typical of their age, could not share. She had developed a game to deal with this. One little girl in particular, a favorite of hers since she was both the child of a good friend and a bright, winsome little person, could not share. When she played with dolls in the dollhouse, moving the tiny pieces of furniture around, if another child came to the area and took some small item, even though Susan was not holding it at the moment, she would push the other child away, with a loud, forceful, "No. No. Mine. Mine. Go away." If it was already in the other's hands, she would pull it away and hold it against her chest with two clenched little fists. If the other child persisted, Susan would let out a loud wail and stamp her feet. Nellie and her assistant, aware of this, had devised a game. Each time they saw a child approaching Susan, they began to clap their hands and call out, "Sharing time, it's sharing time. Olga is going to join Susan and Susan is going to share," and the whole class would clap and sing a song about sharing that Nellie and Rita, her assistant, had composed, Nellie singing while Rita accompanied her on the piano.

Nellie would then go to Susan and, bending over close to her level, say, "What would you like to share with Olga now?" and help her hand the item to Olga. Nellie would give Susan a big hug and kiss and put her on her lap for special time. In time, little Susan learned to share.

THE ANSWER CAME

But Fred was an adult and fixed in his ways. What could she do? The answer came. One day Fred went food shopping, something he had been doing more and more lately, which he seemed to enjoy. While Nellie did not always appreciate his choices of poor quality, she thanked him and said nothing. After a fish dinner one evening, Nellie suddenly became very ill with acute nausea and cramps. Doubled over, she could barely speak. Fred, practically carrying her, rushed her to the hospital emergency room. She was suffering from food poisoning. After she had queried Fred as to where he had bought the fish, the doctor said that others who had purchased fish in that store had also fallen seriously ill. One had died. Recuperating after a few days, Nellie asked Fred why he had bought fish at that particular store rather than the one they usually used. He took a moment before answering and then said, "Because they had a sale and I thought we could save some money." Nellie knew at once that she had to do something drastic. They would consult with their close friend Ephraim, a pious man who knew much and whom both respected. They told their stories to him. Ephraim paid close attention as Fred detailed his anxieties about money and his need to keep tight control. Ephraim smiled and said:

> Fred, when a man departs from this world, neither silver, nor gold, nor precious stones, nor pearls escort him, but only Torah study and good deeds. When you walk, it shall guide you. When you lie down, it shall guard you and when you awake, it shall speak on your behalf.[10]

Ephraim paused and moved his chair closer to Fred's:

> Of course, none of us, including myself, is perfect. But the only way we can change is to carefully observe our actions, watch them, and remove those that are bad habits or troublesome traits.[11] To do this, we need some time for solitude, a time to reflect upon the true path. I think, Fred, that you are afraid. Of what, I am not sure. But sometimes that gets in the way. It is said, for example, that we may become afraid of what time may bring. We may be afraid of cold, heat, accidents, illness—all these things. I think this may be happening to you. To get rid of that is not so hard. Trust in God and do good. That will help us perfect ourselves.

Ephraim laughed. "I didn't mean to give such a long speech but frankly, I hate to see my two dear friends in trouble. I hope I have helped."

Nellie and Fred thanked Ephraim and left. Nellie was quiet, hoping and praying that Ephraim's advice had helped. Fred seemed pensive and into himself.

Nellie waited a few days before referring to their visit with their friend Ephraim. Then she approached Fred: "Fred, I know you're very busy right now with tax season, but I'd like to ask you something. Someone needs an answer. In this morning's mail there was a request for a donation. I would like us to contribute. It is a cause

---

10. *Pirkei Avos, Ethics of the Fathers*, Commentary by Rabbi Moshe Lieber (Brooklyn, NY: Mesorah Publications, 1995), p. 435.

11. Moshe Chaim Luzzato, *The Path of the Just* (Jerusalem: Feldheim Publishing, 1966), pp. 37–43.

I believe in. I'm sure you do, too. Here is the letter. What do you think?" She stood by patiently, waiting as Fred read it. He looked up and seemed to carefully choose his words. "Nellie, I now realize that I have spent so much time worrying about things that really don't exist that I almost feel—what is the word?—foolish. So much wasted energy. I see now that I must make a change for myself, for you, for our marriage and our future. And the best way to do that is to take action. Now. So, Nellie"—Fred put his arm around her—"let's begin with a contribution of $500.00. Is that OK with you? If I'm going to make the change, I may as well begin with a tall order. Maybe that will balance my account in the long run." Nellie had to fight back tears. She hugged her husband. "I can't begin to tell you how happy you've made me. You're a brave and wonderful man." Fred took out his checkbook and sent the check. A few days later, a thank-you arrived. Nellie was the first to open the mail. When Fred returned from work later that day and went into the bedroom to hang up his jacket, there was the thank-you letter beautifully framed and hanging on the wall near their bed. Fred chuckled: "Nellie, we may need a larger room. This may be just the beginning."

And so, as with Hatzlalfonee, a wife on a higher spiritual level than her husband, but eager to please him, can direct him in loving, considerate, and creative ways. Later that night in her most intense moments of intimacy with her husband, Nellie conceived their firstborn child.

❧ 13 ☙

Hannah: Persevering

Abraham and Sarah are the first Jewish couple to enter the path
that would lead to the formation of a new nation on earth, a
nation that would be designated as the major source of earth-con-
nected divinity throughout the Middle East and Western countries.
Their marriage may well be the model for two other marriages, significant in their own ways and influential in Jewish biblical history
as well. In the time frame they are, before the monarchy, Elkanah
and Hannah, and after the monarchy, Mordecai and Esther.

IN A PERIOD OF DECADENCE AND TORPOR

Elkanah fits the model of masculine energy that is thrusting and
goal-oriented. We are talking now about a period of decadence and
general torpor. Although the temple stood at Shiloh, an obsession
with private altars contributed to the abandonment of Shiloh. It was
Elkanah who contributed to religious sensibilities that were otherwise dormant. It is said that he visited the temple four times a year,
always taking his entire family. With serious forethought, he managed to stop along the long way to Shiloh to spread the word that
they were going "to the house of the Lord in Shiloh, whence Torah
and commandments and good deeds emanate. Why not join us?
Let us go together!" And the people would weep and say, "We will
go up with you."[1]

---

1. Rabbi Yehoshua Bachrach, "Elkanah and the Sanctuary of Shiloh,"
Jewish Thought, 1:1 (1990), pp. 2–28.

The heavenly reward Elkanah was given for bringing merit to Israel this way was Samuel. The son of Elkanah and Hannah, Samuel was the prophet and judge who anointed the first Kings in Israel, paving the way for monarchy and the construction of the major temple in Jerusalem. Elkanah aroused interest in the temple, in the Torah, and in God. He fathered Samuel. But, without an appropriate wife, this would have been impossible. Abraham could not have fathered the great Isaac without a wife who experienced God in every fiber of her being. So it was with Isaac and with Jacob; without Rebecca, Jacob could not have mastered the role of Esau along with his own tasks of spirituality. And so it is with children born to parents who contribute to their spiritual development, making an impact lasting beyond old age. In the story of Hannah, we see the characteristics the mother of a king maker must have, particularly when the king must lead a people deep in the throes of inertia, a people descending into spiritual decadence.

We might say that God "needed"—although God has no needs—a vessel. He needed a strong, deep, wide, sturdy, and trustworthy vessel to carry a seed, nurse it, and provide the foundation for a man fit to anoint the first and second kings of Israel. She would have to have a deep and lasting desire, a longing that could sustain eighteen years of barrenness, of humiliation, of frustration. She would need the dedication and persistence of Sarah; the ability to strive for what is right in spite of rejection of Tamar; the clarity and courage of Zipporah; the persistence of Ruth; and the readiness to rise above rejection, humiliation, even mockery. This vessel was Hannah.

The story of Hannah is told in Samuel I,[2] beginning with the description of her husband Elkanah. "He had two wives: the name of the one was Hannah and the name of the second was Peninnah. And Peninnah had children, but Hannah had no children." Shortly after that, we read that when they went up to the temple at Shiloh, Elkanah gave Hannah the choice portion of the peace offerings "for he loved Hannah." And Hannah's rival, the second wife, would offend and anger Hannah, "for the Lord had shut up her womb."[3]

---

2. *The Book of Samuel* 1, trans. Rabbi Rosenberg (New York: The Judaica Press, 1976), 1:1–2. All quotations are taken from this edition.

3. *The Book of Samuel* 1, 1:5.

CRUEL WORDS TEAR A PERSON'S HEART

Year after year, mockery after mockery, Hannah suffered, because she was barren and because she was taunted by Peninnah. "Did you buy your older son a cloak today, or your younger son a shirt?"— thus the second wife would taunt Hannah, reminding her of her childlessness. Our rabbis explain that Peninnah taunted Hannah in order to make her "storm" so that she herself might pray for a child. For eighteen years Hannah relied solely on the prayers of her husband that she bear a child.[4] We see that good intentions are never sufficient; the words we use are central. Kind words of comfort and support could well have brought Hannah to prayer earlier but cruel words, despite the intention behind them, tear a person's heart. Nevertheless, anguished though Hannah was, she never gave up. Her desire to serve God and the Jewish people by having a son who would reflect her own dedication never abated.

SEVEN LAWS LEARNED FROM HANNAH'S PRAYER

Like Moses and like Elijah the prophet, Hannah "hurled words against the Lord," because she knew that to reveal the majesty of God on earth would legitimize her very existence:

> Lord of the Universe, You created two hosts in Your world. The heavenly beings do not multiply, neither do they die, while the earthly beings both multiply and die. If I am of the earthly beings, let me multiply, and if I am of the heavenly beings, let me not die.[5]

Hannah is the first person in the Bible to address God as "Lord of Hosts" (*Tzavaos*)—a God Who has full power over nature, and over the existence of two worlds: the spiritual and the physical. While praying, she wept, clearly praying from the heart and giving deep thought to her prayer.[6] From her prayers and encounter with Eli the priest, the rabbis have learned seven important laws for the

---

4. *The Book of Samuel* 1, note 6, pp. 5–6.
5. *The Book of Samuel* 1, 1:11, notes pp. 7–8.
6. *The Book of Samuel* 1, 1:13.

silent, very holy part of Jewish *davening* (formal prayer), the *Amidah* prayer that is recited three times each day by observant Jews:

> 1) One must direct the heart to God. 2) Frame the words distinctly with the lips. 3) Whisper. 4) One must not be drunk. 5) One must reprove another who does something unseemly. 6) One who is wrongly suspected must clear himself. 7) One who wrongly suspects another of a fault must appease him, and beg his pardon.[7]

Three of the laws are learned from the way Hannah prayed. Four are learned from the encounter that is described below. To appreciate what follows, we need to remember that Hannah remained barren for eighteen years, continuing to depend on the prayers sent up by her husband. Suddenly, a day came when she realized that her dear husband had given up hope of her ever having a child. Imagine her pain. Another woman might well have sunk into despair, "reduced to the dust and ashes that populate the section of our hearts reserved for broken dreams."[8] Not Hannah. As soon as she heard her husband ask, "Hannah, why do you weep? And why do you not eat? And why is your heart sad? Am I not better to you than ten sons?"[9], she herself began to pray for a child, fervently, silently, intensely. Now Eli the priest was watching her pray silently, pointing to various parts of her body as she addressed God, asking, for example, why He gave her breasts if she had no child to nurse. Incorrectly, Eli decided that Hannah must be drunk and he accused her of this. She replied:

> No, My lord, I am a woman of sorrowful spirit, and neither new nor old wine have I drunk, and I poured out my soul before the Lord.[10]

7. "Berakoth," *Zera'im*, *The Babylonian Talmud*, trans. Rabbi I. Epstein (London: The Soncino Press, 1978), pp.191–192.

8. Rebbetzin Tzipporah Heller, "The Light of Awareness," *Hamodia* (May 21, 1999), p.75.

9. *The Book of Samuel* 1, 1:8.

10. *The Book of Samuel* 1, 1:15.

A REMARKABLE SON IS GIVEN

Eli responds well: "Go in peace, and the God of Israel will grant your request, which you have asked of Him." And so the Lord remembered Hannah; the gift of a remarkable son is given to her and to Elkanah, her holy husband.[11]

Hannah named her son Samuel, which means "I asked him of the Lord." Since she had promised to give her son to the service of God, Hannah brought him to the priest as soon as he was weaned. Samuel had great clarity for his age; he was only two or three years old when Hannah gave him over to Eli as his teacher. At one point Samuel even corrected the priest on a matter of slaughtering the sacrifice. Since the boy had the soul of a man of twenty, he would be liable to death at the hands of heaven for humiliating his religious superior. But Hannah, on the spot, pleaded with Eli—"For this child did I pray, and the Lord granted me my requests, which I asked of Him."[12] As a result, the child was saved.

Like Hagar, the second wife, Peninnah, learns her lesson. Little is known about the details of the lives of the two women who harassed their holy superiors; Torah is sparse in its description of negativity but expansive when showing us the way of the righteous. In the story of Hannah, we are inspired to develop our potential for hope, for patience, and for trust. We are inspired to rise above or beyond the mockery of others who, though well meaning, are hurtful nevertheless. We can choose light over whatever darkness seems to surround us. We can study and remember our models: beginning with Sarah and moving on to the women throughout the Bible who chose hope over despair, and action over passivity.

At times change seems to come about through thunder and lightning, torrential rains sweeping everything clean. At other times, one is suddenly in a true altered state of consciousness, not drug-induced but, rather, arising out of the ordinary in an extraordinary way.

---

11. *The Book of Samuel* 1, 1:17.

12. *The Book of Samuel* 1, 1:21–27, note 27, p.13.

LILA WAS TWENTY-ONE AND RESTLESS

Lila was twenty-one and restless. A strong, determined woman, she was unexpectedly feeling a sense of disquiet, her usual clarity and decisiveness blurred. When she was a child, her mother used to say, "Lila, I have never seen anyone as determined as you. If you don't get in through the front door, you go through the back door. You always get to where you want to go. A remarkable quality! I don't know where that came from. It will do you well in life." And it did—until now. Suddenly boyfriends were out of sync with what she wished, her years of training to become a teacher were appreciated but uncentered, life had lost its high; although she was not depressed as it is usually interpreted, something was amiss.

Sharon and Nathan were good parents and appreciative of their daughter. Active in the political arena and contributing time and monies to their particular causes, they lived the life of assimilated Jews. Jewishness was acknowledged but not taken seriously. The "here and now" of contemporary American society was their focus and they blended well into it. But communities were changing. The Cohens, an Orthodox Jewish family, moved next door. Lila became good friends with one of their daughters, called by her Hebrew name, Chayah, or lovingly, Chayele. Although Lila had been closest to two other friends, Debra and Margie, she began to spend more and more time with Chayah. Margie and Debra, aware of this, expressed it: "Lila, is there something we are doing wrong? Whenever we call, you seem preoccupied. And we miss our doing things together. We loved hanging out with you, going to discos, meeting cool guys, having a beer or two, even thinking of getting our tongues pierced. But you seem far away. We're worried. Are you OK? Is there something we should know?" Lila did not know how to explain what was still unclear to her. She said, "There's nothing wrong with you two guys. I really love you. I don't know. I'm just not in the mood to do these things. It's not you, it's me. Be patient." But Lila knew, in her heart of hearts, that this was a half-truth. In a different space, she could no longer relate with passion to their involvements.

IT ALL BEGAN ONE NIGHT

It all began one night at Chayele's house. She was invited to a Sabbath evening dinner. This was totally new to her. From her mother, she was aware that her maternal grandmother had been a practicing Jew in "the old country," but her mother, born in America, had never kept that tradition. Nor had her father who seemed even less interested.

Walking into the Cohen's home was like entering a palace. Candles blazed on elegant candleholders. The table was covered in a crisp, white damask tablecloth; family portraits filled the room: grandparents and great-grandparents, elderly men, rabbis with clear eyes and long beards, young women in long modest dresses. Lila was awed at the solemn beauty, the purity. Close to tears of joy, she sat down at the table where she was welcomed by Rabbi Cohen, Chayah's father. The evening began. It was, for Lila, a meeting of heaven and earth. Learning how to wash her hands, when to speak, when to be quiet, listening for the first time in her life to the prayers and songs sung on the Sabbath, and experiencing the serenity of the night as hour after hour went by, she felt a solemn peace descend upon her, cloaking her in its velvet embrace. She knew now what she had to do: she wished to continue this mode of life.

LILA TURNS TO HER ESSENTIAL BEING

How could Lila tell her parents? Would she be losing them while gaining what was now so essential to her? How could she break away from dear friends and her former lifestyle? But her path was clear. She was determined to follow it. She thought of a plan and, with her usual lucidity, knew that she would have to take one "baby step" at a time. First, she must learn to pray. She would attend the synagogue with Chayah, and it would be her first time ever in a synagogue. Her friend was delighted and they went together for Sabbath services. Chayah handed her the *Siddur* (the book of prayers) and said that she could follow it in English. Lila stood very close to Chayah, watching her every move. She copied her friend. Not yet understanding what was happening, she was nonetheless captured by the atmosphere, the sense of awe, of dedication and purpose. The women responded as a body to words spoken or sung by the men. Their voices were full and rich, traveling upward, as if to reach Heaven, Lila thought. She learned the different names of God and how He was revealed or concealed based upon humankind's relationship to Him. A new world had opened its portals to her and she, eager and naive newcomer, was in ecstasy.

She shared her experience with her mother. Sharon was contemplative and said, "I knew something was wrong, but I didn't know what. I'm glad you found what you want. But, honey, you have to understand. From everything I've heard, and I think it must be true, it's very hard to be a Jew. There seem to be so many rituals, so many do's and don'ts. Do you think you really want to travel this road? I mean, I don't want to dissuade you, but is this something you can do? I know I couldn't. And I can't speak for your papa, but I don't think he could either." She gave a short laugh. "He wouldn't know where to start. And frankly, neither would I." Lila replied, "Mama, I feel strongly that this is what I must do. I know little as yet, but I don't see any of this as just ritual. It is not something I do as an exercise, or an obligation. What I felt at the Cohens' house last week on that glorious night and what I experienced at the synagogue was a feeling of nearness to God, or at least a beginning of that. Chayah told me that He is available to us here on earth, that we can talk to Him as a friend. And that night, Mama dear, after I went home and before I went to sleep, I opened the book Chayah lent me, the book with all the prayers, and I prayed. And somehow, deep within me, I knew God was listening. I know this may sound crazy, but He seemed to be in the room, right there with me." Sharon said not a word. She just kissed her daughter on her forehead and wished her a good night.

"I DON'T UNDERSTAND WHAT YOU'RE DOING."

Lila told her best friends, Debra and Margie, about her experiences at the Sabbath dinner and at the synagogue. Debra said, "I love you, Lila. We've been friends since we were kids in elementary school. But I don't understand what you're doing. I mean, you're cutting out such a large part of your life. You're going to have to wear all those strange-looking clothes. They look out of the last century, if not earlier, not to mention no makeup, probably no sexy lingerie, all the other unmentionables. You'll have to give all that up. Do you really want to? What will happen to us? We were always such a terrific threesome."

"I love you both," said Lila. "And I would not like to give you up. I don't have to. We could see each other. I will respect your ways if you respect mine. Of course, you could also give it a shot and try going to the synagogue once or twice. Who knows? You may find something there, too. But, even if you don't, your friendship is of value to me. I would like to keep it." Debra and Margie hugged Lila and said, "Well, dear friend, we think you're a little nuts, but go and do what you need to. You will anyway. You always have. It is one of your best qualities, you know. And if we meet an Orthodox guy hanging around anywhere, we'll be sure to send him your way."

LILA BEGINS HER JOURNEY

And so Lila began her journey. She was going the whole way. "If I'm going to do it," she said, "I'm going to do it right." She got a job teaching at one of the local schools. Now self-employed and earning her own money, she had a long talk with her parents. She would find a small apartment somewhere in the neighborhood or a room in the house of an observant family, so that she could learn from them. She would begin serious study. Chayah helped her. Together, they checked out the talks given on different subjects relating to Judaism, books Lila could begin reading, and books she must buy. She followed her instructions down to the smallest detail. Going over her wardrobe, she made changes, discarding some items and buying others of a more modest nature to replace them. She toned down her makeup, but learned that single women did not cover their hair. She read voraciously, drinking in what she found in the writings and digesting it fully. Her restlessness gave way to a feeling of calm as she began to understand and deeply feel that all that came her way was for the better. Despite the gentle teasing by Margie and Debra, she did not veer from her chosen path. Her parents accepted her mode of life but did not participate in it. They listened to her, but suspected that this was just a "phase she is going through, like when she was determined to be a ballet dancer at twelve." But Lila's persistence and dedication were real. When she felt some doubt, she prayed to God with fervor and passion, talking to Him as women talk to a beloved friend. And He, in His infinite goodness, sent light to dissipate the darkness. Lila, in reciprocity and gratitude, thanked Him ever the more, her perseverance, like Hannah's, never faltering.

✥ 14 ✥

Three Women: Abigail, Huldah, Esther

ABIGAIL: PURE AND BEAUTIFUL WITHIN AND WITHOUT

We have seen how a number of outstanding Biblical women open the way to appropriate behavior at crucial moments, instructing husband, father, or priest, and molding the future of Israel according to God's plan. Because the range of relationships in which Biblical women are involved is wide, we need now to explore three women who had to cope with men of might and power: Abigail, Huldah, and Esther.[1] The men of might are David, king of Israel; Josiah, king of Israel; and Achasuerus, king of Persia.

ABIGAIL WAITS TO DISCOVER HER PURPOSE

We meet Abigail at a time when David, anointed to become the next king, is not yet on the throne. The sitting king of Israel, Saul filled

---

1. *The Book of Samuel 1*, trans. Rabbi A.J. Rosenberg (New York: The Judaica Press, 1976), 25: 25–31, pp. 212–214. *The Book of Kings 2*, trans. Rabbi A.J. Rosenberg (New York: The Judaica Press, 1980), chapter 22. *II Chronicles, The Tanach*, The Artscroll Series, Stone Edition, ed. Nosson Scherman (Brooklyn, New York: Mesorah Publications, 1996), 34:19ff. *The Book of Esther, The Megillah*, 2nd ed., trans. Rabbi Meir Zlotowitz (Brooklyn, NY: Mesorah Publications, 1976). Unless otherwise specified, all quotations in this chapter are drawn from these texts.

with jealousy, seeks to kill David who is now on the run from him. Abigail, known by all to be understanding, pure, and beautiful within and without, is married to Nabal, a selfish man of evil deeds. He is called great only because he is very rich and of noble lineage. Abigail does all she can as a wife but cannot influence her husband for the better. Although she can end the marriage, she does not. Perhaps, like Esther, sensing a divine purpose for her marriage, Abigail waits patiently to discover what that purpose might be.[2]

Our story begins when David arrives in Nabal's territory. Knowing that it is a time of sheepshearing when the custom was to make a banquet for the sheepshearers, David sends some of his men to ask for whatever food Nabal can give to them. They had been guarding his sheep, showing great respect for his shepherds. Naval responds with scorn, "Who is David, and who is the son of Jesse? Nowadays, there are many slaves, who break away, each one from his master." In short, he refuses to share any of his food with David and his men.

Such effrontery cannot go unpunished. David commanded "Gird each man with his sword. And David and four hundred of his men girded their swords!"[3] Meanwhile, Abigail is warned by one of the servants, "And now go and see what you will do, for the evil has been decided upon against our master and against all of his household; and he is such a base person that one cannot speak to him."[4]

True to her reputation, Abigail hastens, taking two hundred loaves, jugs of wine, prepared sheep, flour, clusters of raisins, and cakes of figs to be sent to David at once. Telling her husband nothing, she rides on her donkey, coming down the mountain to meet David and his four hundred men on their way to destroy all that belongs to the household of Nabal. Abigail prostrates herself on the ground falling at the feet of David to say, "In me alone, my lord, is the iniquity."[5]

---

2. *The Book of Samuel 1*, 25:3–5, note 3 page 206. *"Megillah," Mo'ed 4, The Babylonian Talmud*, trans. Maurice Simon (London: The Soncino Press, 1978), p. 84.

3. *The Book of Samuel 1*, 250–11, notes 10–11, pp. 208ff.

4. *The Book of Samuel 1*, 25:13, note 13 p. 209, and 25:14–17.

5. *The Book of Samuel 1*, 25:18–20; 25:23–24.

ABIGAIL'S PLEA IS A MIGHTY ONE

Her plea is a mighty one. Using all the powers of persuasion given to women, Abigail convinces David that his plan of action is based on faulty reasoning because, although he has been anointed by heavenly decree as king of Israel, David is not yet seated on his earthly throne:

> Let not my lord take heed of this base fellow, of Nabal, for like his name, so is he. Nabal is his name, and ungratefulness is with him; and I, your handmaid, did not see my lord's youths that you sent. And now, my lord, as the Lord lives and by your life, I swear that the Lord has withheld you from coming to bloodshed, and from saving yourself with your hand. And now, may your enemies and those who seek evil to my lord, be as Nabal. And now, this gift, which your handmaid has brought to my lord, shall be given to the youths who walk at my lord's feet. Forgive now your handmaid's transgression, for the Lord shall make for my lord a sure house, for my lord fights the wars of the Lord. And let no evil be found in you all your days. And a man has arisen to pursue you and to seek your soul. But my lord's soul shall be bound in the bundle of life with the Lord your God, while the soul of your enemies, the Lord will sling it with the hollow of the sling. And it will be, when the Lord will do to my lord according to all the good which He spoke concerning you, and He will appoint you as ruler over Israel. Let this not be to you as a stumbling block and remorse of heart to my lord, that you have shed blood without cause, or that my lord has avenged himself. And when the Lord will do good to my lord, you shall remember your maidservant.[6]

David's response is very positive. He blesses the Lord God of Israel Who has sent her to him and he blesses Abigail as well as her advice, saying, "See that I have hearkened to your voice and have shown you favor."[7]

---

6. *The Book of Samuel 1*,25:25–31, notes 25–31, pp. 212–214.

7. *The Book of Samuel 1*, 25:32–35.

David's restraint is echoed in Abigail; when she returns to her home to find Nabal very drunk, she tells him nothing. The next morning when she does tell him all that has occurred, he becomes like stone. Ten days later he dies.

David sends for her to become his wife. Bringing five maidens with her, she hastens to become the wife of David.[8]

Clearly, like Esther, Abigail humbles herself before a king. Although David is not yet king on earth, as prophetess, Abigail knows what is to come and submits totally to this truth. Unlike Esther, however, she is humbling herself before a very great man, one beloved of God. In her plea to David to restrain from killing her husband, there are six references to herself as his handmaid. Abigail prostrates herself on the ground when she meets David for the first time and again when she responds to the servants who come to her with the message, "David has sent us to you to take you to him for a wife."[9]

Like Huldah and Deborah, Abigail is faulted on one point in her response to David. At the end of her plea that saved David from shedding blood without cause, Abigail asks him to remember her when he is king.[10] We can sympathize with Abigail. After years of living patient and kind with a vile husband, what woman would not wish to marry the great man who has taken her good advice and blessed her as well? Nevertheless, just as much is expected of outstanding men who are put to the test (Abraham, Isaac, Jacob, Moses, and others), much is expected of great women as well.

The two men in the life of Abigail epitomize the dimensions of evil and good. While good represents perfection, only God is true perfection. His wisdom decrees that giving humans the opportunity to attach themselves to Him makes it possible for them to reach for perfection. Moving away from our deficiencies, we can consciously choose goodness as a means of attaching ourselves to God.

---

8. *The Book of Samuel 1*, 25:37–38, notes 37–38, pp. 216–217.

9. *The Book of Samuel 1*, 25:40–41.

10. *The Book of Samuel 1*, 25:31. "*Megillah*," p. 84.

God created the concepts of perfection and deficiency as well as a creature (mankind) with equal access to both.[11]

ABIGAIL'S HUSBAND IS SELF-INFLATED

Naval is portrayed as evil, self-inflated, and arrogant. However, knowing that there is a reason for everything, Abigail remained in the marriage. He dies after she tells him what must have severely stressed him. In modern terms we suggest that he may have been a Type A personality, characterized by aggressiveness, extreme impatience, anxiety, and high susceptibility to stress; these characteristics could have led to the stroke that led to the death of Naval.

Contemporary women, in long- or short-term marriages, may not experience their husbands as vile or mean as Naval. But there are personality traits that get in the way of harmony in a marriage. Husbands need not be extreme or abusive. When they are, many women choose to leave. Balanced with the good qualities, other qualities are more subtle and entrenched. Even when good qualities are few, most women forgive, willing to focus on the good, and knowing, as did Abigail, that negative traits may mirror qualities potentially within ourselves. Visible in the other, they make us even more sensitive to our ability to choose.

CHARACTER TRAITS THAT PROVOKE STRESS

What are some of the character traits in a spouse that provoke stressors in our everyday existence? From our clinical files and composite profiles of clients, we list personality types particularly that are difficult to live with:[12]

---

11. Moshe Chaim Luzzato, *The Way of God* (Jerusalem and New York: Feldheim, 1983), p. 39.

12. Basic Behavioral Science Task Force of the National Advisory Mental Health Council, "Vulnerability and Resilience," *American Psychologist* 51:1 (January, 1996), 22–28.

1. The Reactor

This type overreacts to everyone and everything. When he does, it is explosive. He goes from one to ten in a blazing moment. Unable to modulate his responses, he erupts. Yet, in a short time, he can settle down as though tranquillity is his specialty. Once a lion, he is now a lamb, convinced that the one who is the object of his outbursts is somewhat delusional or just "too sensitive." A typical woman's response is:

> I never know when he is going to fly off the handle. One day I can say something and nothing happens. The next time there is this volcano spewing flames right in front of me. I can't wait to get away, to run from the storm. When I do, he pursues me, wanting to know what's wrong. I can't believe it. The change is so automatic, almost as if it didn't happen. But it did. It takes me a while to reach my equilibrium again. I don't think he understands how this creates problems in our marriage. I don't want to leave him, the children, the house, the community, everything. But frankly I don't know what to do. If only he had more control.

Can the overreactor change? For several decades, research on human development has emphasized the stability of personality traits throughout the life span. However, more recently, social scientists have concluded that "discontinuity rather than continuity best characterizes lives over time." Intrinsic to this is the ability to make changes in behavior. Change can take place at any time and at any age.[13] What is needed is motivation, willingness on the part of the person exhibiting the behavior, and an environment that is supportive and rewarding.

For the Reactors, learning to feel the cues to what disturbs them— in other words, putting a lid on the explosion before it reaches full steam—can be an enormous help. A wife can help, empathetically pointing out what she sees as his danger triggers. She must do this without blame and anger, no easy task but a necessary one if she wishes to promote healing. Another approach may be to walk away

---

13. Robert A. Nemiroff, *New Dimensions in Adult Development*, ed. Calvin A. Colarusso (New York: Basic Books, 1990), pp. 215–263.

as the explosion surfaces. This leaves the husband without an audience, and aloneness may help him to turn inward rather than outward, his usual mode.

2. The Blamer

The Blamer does just that: pointing the finger away from himself, he directs the blame toward others: "It's all your fault, you made me do it. If you hadn't done . . . it would never have happened."

Similar to the Reactor, the Blamer is afraid to peer into his own interior. To do so fills him with terror. What could be hiding there? Is he really guilty? Why open this Pandora's box filled with the unknown? It's much safer to look outside himself. That's visible. No hidden danger there. How can his spouse deal with this?

We do not know which type of man Abigail's husband, Naval, was although he was known to be hateful to all. But for persons with personality deficiencies, peeling away the obvious behavioral styles, as noxious as they are, results in hurt, pain, fear, and terror. They learned, probably in their earlier years, that a suit of armor was the most viable in their particular setting. And it was. Now that they are mature, it is no longer so, but they may not know how to make the change.

Again, we do not know how Abigail handled the stress of living with a man with characterological problems. But, strong, independent, creative, and flexible as she was, she remained a good wife in every way possible.

3. The Charmer

Not easy to target, the Charmer is typically loved by all except those who have to live with him. Delightful, humorous, polite, with a fluid, easy style of living, he is simply charming. Yet, on familiar territory such as home and hearth, his true nature is revealed. This may take many turns: he can be nasty, uncaring, insensitive, stingy, mean, and totally self-involved once his major audience, outside of his close family, is no longer present. Without an audience of admirers, why need the performer perform? Again, while this style was acquired early on, it can be changed. If he was raised in a family where external values were stressed, where one lived to please others, where appearances were the focus and the interiority of the person a desert, then who you are, what you feel, and how you behave are directed outside the self. You are a slick form of hype for all to see.

Difficult for the wife is that, because of the smoothness of this person, it is hard to prick his skin. He seldom bleeds, except for those rare times when his desperation surfaces, when his emptiness of self leaves him feeling, for just a moment, like a painted shell: fragile, unreal, and totally vulnerable. It is precisely at those times that his wife can offer empathy in both words and actions. Not seduced by his external charm, she can show him that, despite his faulty image of self and lack of trust, he can change, he is worthy, he does, indeed, have an interior. She has caught glimpses of it and loves what she sees. Coaxing, she can urge him to find truth and beauty in connecting to God, and this attachment will supply him with all he needs.

By sensitively choosing her actions and words, she can help him move away from false glitter to the profound depths we were given in the beginning.

4. *The Separatist*

The Separatist does not make connections. All aspects of his life are seen and lived as though separate from one another. For example, he may consider himself spiritual and religious, and he may well be. But parts of his life are lived in disharmony with this image. He uses his rationalization to defend this: "business is business," he may declare when accused of dishonesty. If he has an addiction—like alcohol, gambling, or womanizing—he may explain it away. He does not see these actions as interfering with dedication to his faith. When his wife complains about his attachment to negative and destructive behavior, he tells her, "It has nothing to do with you. I am a good husband, father, and provider. I don't know what you are complaining about." Indeed, he does not. With her innate powers of persuasion, a wife may show her husband that we are created in God's image and the image is one, not two, three, or four. Our wholeness of being and the way we live can emulate the attributes shown us by the Almighty.

Naval is known to have had a glorified image of himself. Some men do. This is their type:

5. The King

A monarch without a throne, he acts as though he has one. All are there to serve him. His words, actions, and thoughts are not to be disputed. He has, and is, the final word. All-knowing, he does not believe that the Creator knows all, plans all, and sees all. He may not intentionally dispute this, for he considers himself a man of faith, but his rule is not to be questioned. If others do not obey him, follow his orders explicitly, or offer interpretations other than his, they tread on shaky ground. A woman living with such a man tells this story:

> He is, I know, a very smart man, and very successful in business. But it is like living with a tyrant. He dismisses all I say as not important, sometimes even stupid and certainly unsophisticated. He tells me what to do as though I were his child, not his wife and equal. Yes, he is generous, but I have no rights. I do not feel free enough to make judgments from my own heart. I hate to say this, but somehow I have become intimidated. I have, in his eyes, been wrong so many times, that I no longer trust myself. Even with the children, while he does say, with appreciation, that I am an excellent mother, I now go to him with all kinds of problems and he, I have to admit, makes all the decisions. I don't know how it happened, but my trust in myself has, slowly but surely, withered. I am a shadow of who I once was.

Naval was a man who, contrary to God's will, did only what he wanted to do. Clearly, Abigail knew that the King was not, in truth, a monarch, but rather one who incorrectly feels that he is in charge of others. What he believes and does is not truth, but a made-up story, arising from his own deficiencies. His overdramatization of self-importance is the layering for a poor self-image and diluted self-esteem.

A CARING WIFE LOOKS PAST THE FACADE

A caring wife can look past the facade, bolster the husband's intrinsic self, and nurture him with kind firmness, not allowing herself to be seduced by his vanities. Standing firm on her own ground may help dissolve some of the delusions he has about himself. As with our Charmer, the monarch without a kingdom is no longer a king. The wife must, without anger but with compassion, offer the reassurance that he need not be a king for her to love him. However, what Abigail did to help Naval did not serve to change him. The Bible presents a number of different marital possibilities, but this is one where even the best of women cannot change her husband at all.

Abigail's suffering with Naval is rewarded. She becomes the second wife of David. The well-known feats of David will not be detailed here, but Jewish tradition tells us that the Messiah will descend from the House of David. Both warrior and singer, David played the harp with fervor. His capacity to feel deeply is exemplified in his mourning the death of Jonathan, his trusted friend: "How the mighty have fallen in the midst of battle. Oh, Jonathan, you were slain in the high places. I am distressed for you, my brother, you were very pleasant to me. Your love for me was more wonderful than the love of woman."[14] Love and passion are signs of a developed personality, confirming our deep, often consuming, connection to another. Limited is the person who lacks the ability to bond. Long before he became king on an earthly throne, Abigail knew the greatness of David.

HULDAH SPARKED A GREAT SPIRITUAL REVIVAL

With the help of Abigail, David became king of Israel. After David's death, King Solomon built the first temple in Jerusalem. But the golden age of Jewish monarchy did not last. Friction, strife, and civil war followed. By 478 BCE, Jewish kings became fanatical pagans. To study the prophetess Huldah, we focus on a period that began with Amon, son of Menesheh. Amon attacked the Jewish religion "with peculiar vindictiveness." Assassinated two years after he ascended the throne, Amon was replaced by his eight-year-old son, Josiah. Although he was raised in a pagan environment, the boy-king came to embrace the faith of his earlier Jewish ancestors. By the time he reached the age of 16, he chose to repair the damage that had been inflicted on the kingdom by both his father and grandfather. In the course of repairing the holy temple, his workers discovered the Torah scroll written by Moses almost one thousand years before. It was open to the section in which God reproves His people: "God shall

---

14. *The Book of Samuel 2*, trans. Rabbi Moshe Ch. Sosevsky (New York: Judaica Press, 1978), I:23.

deport you and the king you appoint for yourselves to a nation un-known to you or your fathers, and you will be subservient to alien gods of wood and stone. And you will be desolate, ridiculed, and mocked by all the peoples wherever God will deliver you."[15]

Weeping, the king sent his high priest and four of his leading men, including the scribe, to consult the prophetess Huldah. Her message "sparked the last great spiritual revival in the Kingdom of Judah."[16]

Who was Huldah? She was a prophetess in Israel and cousin to the great prophet Jeremiah. But why did the king choose to send his men to consult, not Jeremiah, but instead the prophetess Huldah? It is possible that Jeremiah was not there because he was away seeking the ten lost tribes. Others believe it was known that a woman would be more merciful than a man, and therefore Huldah would surely pray for any evil decree to be averted for Josiah and his people. She would show greater compassion than her male coun-terpart. Furthermore, when God shows prophecy through a woman, He is softening the blow that is to come. A woman's way of deliver-ing prophecy becomes more acceptable to the people, for her way of speaking gives hope and encouragement, consolation, and strength.[17]

That Huldah "was sitting in Jerusalem in the study hall" is said to mean that she was teaching the Oral Law to the elders and ex-pounding all the words that are repeated in the Torah. She taught the book known as *Mishneh Torah*, which is Deuteronomy. By ex-pounding on the parts that are repeated, she was illustrating that the laws derived from apparently redundant words are as binding and stringent as those explicitly written.

When the five great men appeared to seek her advice, Hulda responded at once, and this is what she told them:

Say to the man who sent you to me, "So has the Lord said, 'Behold I bring calamity to this place and upon its inhab-

---

15. *The Book of Kings 2*, 21:20ff. Yaakov Yosef Reinman, *Destiny* (Lakewood, New Jersey: Olive Tree Press, 1995), pp.124ff.

16. Reinman, p.125.

17. Ibid., p. 125. "*Megillah*," *Mo'ed* 4, p. 84.

itants. . . . Because they have forsaken Me and have burned
incense to pagan deities, in order to provoke Me with all
the deeds of their hands, My wrath is kindled against this
place, and it shall not be quenched.'" And concerning the
king of Judah who has sent you to inquire of the Lord, so
shall you say to him, "So has the Lord God of Israel said,
'The words are what you heard. Since your heart has become soft, and you have humbled yourself before the Lord,
when you heard what I spoke about this place and about
its inhabitants, to become a desolation and a curse, and
you rent your garments and wept before Me, I, too, have
heard [it]," says the Lord. " 'Therefore, behold I gather you
in to your forefathers, and you shall be gathered into your
graves in peace, and your eyes shall not see any of the
calamity I am bringing upon this place'."[18]

The prophetic words of Huldah revealed beyond doubt that the
people had forsaken the worship of God, had burned incense to
pagan gods and opened the way to terrible destruction to come.
However, Josiah, not involved in these sins, would thus not live to
see the destruction of the Holy Temple and the ensuing exile of the
Jews. Instead he would die before that time and receive a proper
burial.

Huldah's words created a tremendous reformation. The effect
on the king was immediate: "His words rang clear when he bade
them fulfill the laws and carried out his threat 'Cursed be he that
keeps it not!' His brow darkened when those who stood aloof from
the Torah outraged him by compromising with those who rejected
the law and the statutes. Josiah assembled the people from small
to great, and he read the words of the scroll of the covenant. He
had all the utensils that were used to worship foreign gods burned.
Pagan priests were abolished as were houses devoted to pagan
worship.[19]

As is the case with great people, the slightest infraction must be
taken seriously. Thus, like Abigail and Deborah, Huldah is faulted

18. *The Book of Kings 2*, 22:14–20, notes pp. 411–412.
19. *The Book of Kings 2*, 23:1–28. *II Chronicles*, 34:29–31.

for some of her words. She said, "Say to the man who sent you to me." The man was, after all, king of Israel, not an ordinary person. One would need to refer to him at all times as the king.[20]

IS THERE SOMETHING IN HULDAH'S PROPHETIC POWERS THAT HAS FILTERED DOWN TO MODERN TIMES?

Who is elevated to becoming a prophetess? We are told that it "depends chiefly on the will of God who is to prophesy and at what time; and that He only selects the best and the wisest."[21] In addition, while God creates the possibility, it cannot be completed without intense study and training. Is there something in Huldah's prophetic powers that has filtered down from ancient to modern times? Does the modern woman possess inherent powers that render her sensitive to future possibilities? It is our conjecture that a woman's intuition is often the source of such knowledge. But what is intuition and who possesses it? While we all possess this intuitive faculty, we do so in different degrees. We feel our intuitive powers strongly in things we understand well. And some persons are so strong in their imagination and intuitive faculty that, when they assume a thing to be in existence, the reality either entirely or partially confirms their assumptions. Although the causes of this assumption are numerous, by means of the intuitive faculty, the intellect can pass over all these causes and draw inferences from them very quickly, almost instantaneously. This same faculty enables some persons to foretell important coming events.[22]

It is this sixth sense, whose seat is in the heart rather than in the mind or the five senses, that makes a woman particularly sensitive to all that is going on and thus to what the future may hold. If we were to categorize women into two types, at opposite extremes, we could say that some are well defended. Nothing fazes them. They face their outer and inner worlds with ready words and

---

20. *"Megillah", Mo'ed* 4, p. 85. *The Book of Kings 2*, xxii:15.

21. Moses Maimonides, *The Guide for the Perplexed*, 2nd ed., trans. M. Friedlander (New York: Dover, 1956), p. 220.

22. Ibid., pp.224, 229.

actions and do not easily tumble. Reality-bound and grounded, their feet are firmly planted in life. Our society gives much credence to this type, but pays little homage to intuitive types, and little is done to develop our potential for intuition. The intuitive woman shows this capacity early on. She is usually a thinker. Fascinated with ideas and abstractions, she questions and questions—"What is the meaning of life? What is its purpose? Where am I going? How can I best connect to God? What is the path I am to choose? How do I know this?" Trusting what they feel, their inner experiences, and their hearts, they merge feelings and thought to guide their actions. But isn't every woman like that? No. Most of us, rooted to the realities of everyday life, receive information from our five senses. Ours is an empirically oriented society. Despite our religious and spiritual dimensions, we often fall prey to its entrapments. "I need hard evidence to make that decision," says the sensory-oriented type. "Show me and I'll believe it" or "How can you trust your insights? They're only your feelings." The physical world is their reality, no more, no less.

INTUITIVE WOMEN EXPERIENCE LONELINESS

Because of their sensitivity and creativity, qualities that are high in intuitive women, they may experience much loneliness. One woman told her therapist:

> I had started therapy because I was not sure of just about anything. I did believe in God, but sometimes, I could not fathom His ways. I wanted to understand. I also had visions, which I learned not to share with my friends because they just looked at me, thinking that I was weird, strange, or just different. It was a shock to me to hear my therapist, a woman, tell me that I was indeed a most unusual, creative young woman, but because I was so unlike so many others my age, I would experience much loneliness. I was amazed but relieved. I had always felt this sense of aloneness even with my good friends. At parties or large gatherings, I felt so inadequate with the chitchat and cocktail conversation. Usually, I just made some excuse and ran. It was that devastating. But, on some level, I felt like a freak. Not normal. Would I ever be normal?

This young woman wanted depth. It was not until many years later, as a mature adult who was well on the way to becoming a noted artist, that her feelings of difference disappeared. She said, "They say you paint what you see. I don't. I paint what I feel."

WHAT CAN THE INTUITIVE TYPE DO?

What can the intuitive type do? She can find others like herself, and while not rejecting the reality-bound types, acknowledge her uniqueness. One woman did just that:

> When my first son was born, I used to sit outdoors on the little bench we had outside this sweet, old wooden house we had just bought. As soon as some of the other mothers would see me, they would approach. They were nice women. All had babies or young children. We had much in common. But still, I liked sitting there by myself, reading or sometimes just sitting still. My heart was open, my mind ready to receive, and my body relaxed. I would watch a bird land on a tree, listen to his sounds, and trace his journey as he hopped from one tree to another. Or I would watch my son sleeping, in wonder at his perfection: how his tiny little feet were assembled, how soft and light his breath, how deep his sleep. Was he dreaming? Was he aware of how precious he was to me, or of how blessed his father and I felt to have him? I never expressed these thoughts to the other women. But one day I did, to my friend Malka. She burst out laughing. For a moment, I turned to stone. But then she said, "Shiffrah, you too? I thought I was the only one in this world." We hugged and kissed and cried a little. It was pure joy, finding a soul mate. Now, many years later, we are still devoted friends and are totally accepting of our intuitive selves.

THE HEART: A BASE OF INTUITION

The intuitive woman, no longer called a prophetess, can perform amazing feats. Sometimes her feelings seem groundless. What out there matches what in there? But incredibly, at times disaster is avoided when she does listen to her heart, her base of intuition. One woman stood firm in her intuition and was ever grateful for it:

We had planned this trip to my husband's birthplace over-seas at least a year before. He was most anxious to revisit Spain, see his family, and connect to old memories of his childhood. Since we lived in a Sephardic community, we had friends who were also born there. One couple decided to travel with us. We were happy about that. It would be good to have company, and our husbands could share their growing-up experiences together. We arrived at the airport early and watched some planes land and leave. We had our flight-time schedules in our hands. Our plane had come in and was being unloaded. We were told over the loud-speaker that it would soon be ready for boarding. Suddenly, something clutched at my heart. A dark cloud seemed to appear in front of me. In reality, it was a mild, sunny day. My throat closed. I could not breathe. Some terrible warn-ing pounced on the seat of my soul, squeezing me, and forcing me to pay attention. I had had such feelings before and acted on them, but usually I was alone. Could I do this now? It was not only the two of us who were involved, but our friends also. What could I say? I decided to speak out, "We can't take this plane. We'll have to wait for the next one. Or we can change to another airline. That's done sometimes." My friends looked at me, surprise on their faces. "But why?" they asked. "Are you not well? Shall we get a doctor, an ambulance, something to help you?" "No," I said. " I am fine. And I know this sounds crazy, but we cannot take that plane. I can't explain it. I don't know how and why, but that plane is not safe. I just can't go on it and hope you don't either." Well, they probably thought I was a lot stranger than they knew, but as good friends, they were willing to accommodate me. We did not take that plane, and, although it meant several hours of waiting, we took another. Our original plane never made it. Something about a storm, signals not working, damage to a part of the plane. There was a crash. The crew did not survive, nor did most of the passengers except for a baby and its mother who were wounded. What can I say? I thank God Almighty for this ability He gave to me for His own good reasons. If this is the way it was meant to be, I can appreciate this gift within myself and use it for the benefit of others. It is a blessing.

RECOGNIZING OUR INTUITIVE POWERS

Since the destruction of the temple, prophecy has ceased. While intuition is not the same as prophecy, it exists within us, and needs to be recognized and applauded. It comes to us in an instant. To receive it, we may need to lie still each morning for a long moment before jumping up and beginning the day's routine: opening to receptivity and surrounding the self with quiet. Rabbi Meir Fund says, "The first thought that comes to a person is often a heavenly guidance, whereas the rebuttal of that thought represents our own inner anxiety and insecurity."[23]

Our intuition sends us messages from above. Similar to night dreams, which at times point us to the path to take, our day life contains messages as well. The receiver is the heart, storage center for intuition. Opening the self to receive, we may not be Huldah, but a woman's intuition is available to many women. It is our heritage.

ESTHER: MISTRESS OF RESTRAINT

We have seen how Abigail's words saved the throne for King David and how Huldah's prophecy created a religious reformation in Israel. In the period of exile that followed the destruction of the temple, great restraint was needed. A paragon of virtue and mistress of restraint, Queen Esther with the help of her husband, Mordecai, saved the Jewish people from total destruction.[24]

---

23. Rabbi Meir Fund, personal communication (Brooklyn, New York: June 7, 1999).

24. *The Book of Esther.* The *"Megillah," Mo'ed* 4, pp. 75–76.

"And when her father and mother died, Mordecai took her for his own daughter. A Tanna taught in the name of R. Meir: Read not 'for a daughter' (*le-bath*), but 'for a house' (*le-bayith*). . . . it means a wife."

Rashi, "Our Rabbis explained the word (see above) as wife" (Meg. 13a). *The Megilloth and Rashi's commentary with Linear translation*, tr. Rabbi Avraham Schwartz and Rabbi Yisroel Schwartz (New York City: 1983: Hebrew Linear Classics), p. 11 on Esther 2:7.

King David planned the temple that was built after his death by his son Solomon. The Golden Age of Jewish monarchy was followed by strife and divisiveness and finally by the destruction of the temple and the conquest of Israel by Babylonia. The exile stretched out when Persia conquered Babylonia and inherited the Jewish subjects. Exile in Persia ensued. The story of this exile as described in *The Book of Esther* lasted for seventy-two years. Because of an incorrect calculation by Achasuerus, the anti-Semitic king of Persia, it was believed that God had not saved the Jewish people as promised, had not returned them to the Holy Land, and had not restored the temple. "Now," said the king of Persia, "we shall celebrate the demise of the Jewish people." At a banquet that lasted for six months, Achasuerus used the holy utensils of the temple as part of the feast. Everybody had to be pleased. Everybody had to be made happy, happy, happy— an impossible feat on earth, a heretical gesture, a hysterical attempt to play God on earth. The Jews were invited, kosher food was served and, strange to say, except for the chief rabbi, Mordecai, the Jews came. At the banquet an event occurred, which would eventually unleash the power of the conquered people. Until now, they had been squashing their identity, and wallowing in Persian luxury and hedonism. At one point in the six month spree, the king called for Queen Vashti to appear before his men without her clothing so that all could delight in her beauty. Unlike her usual immoral self, Vashti sent a nasty note to her husband, publicly disclaiming his indecency, and comparing him unfavorably to her great father, the former king of Babylonia, who drank far more than did her lowly bred husband, yet never displayed such horrible behavior. It was clear that Achasuerus' rise to fame rested on the high birth and political acumen of his wife, Vashti. What followed was a display of total confusion. Should Vashti be punished? Of course. Should she be executed? Well, the king did not want to lose her. He went to his council for advice, hinting broadly, but clearly, that she should not be executed. By calling her Queen Vashti, rather than Vashti the queen, he knew his wish for her would be clear to the council. However, one of the council members was absent that day. In his place a certain Memuchan, really Haman, appeared and spoke first. Strange, since Persian law insisted that new members did not speak until all the others had spoken. Yet nobody seemed to mind the indecorous, even rebellious, nature of Haman's statements. He argued, "Let us kill the queen. Otherwise all women in the land will overcome the power of their husbands. Furthermore, let us decree that from now on the king has the power to execute anyone that he disapproves of without coming to this Council." Not a single voice was heard in objection to this ridiculous decree. It meant that from now on the members of the council would never have the courage to appear before the king, to offer him advice, or to use their political acumen to help this foolish man rule his vast kingdom. Henceforth, only hairdressers and servants of the king dared to make suggestions to him.[25]

ESTHER, THE NEW QUEEN

Vashti disappeared. It is suggested that she was executed and the king was left to despair, longing for his lost queen. His new advisors suggested that to replace Vashti they hold a beauty contest throughout the land. Ironically, a new queen emerged. She was 60 years old— a Jewish woman descended from the holy family of King Saul. She was radiant with the inner beauty of holiness but not beautiful in appearance. She was Esther, both ward and wife of Mordecai, the chief rabbi of Persia. Strange to say, nobody seemed to know that she was Jewish or married to the chief rabbi. During the ensuing years, Mordecai watched carefully from the courtyard all that happened to his wife in the palace. They sent messages to each other, but nobody noticed. One of the messages from Mordecai to Esther revealed that two traitors were plotting the assassination of the king. Esther shared the news with the king who had the rebels executed.[26]

ESTHER REMAINS SILENT AND PATIENT

During the twelve years since she was kidnapped and raised to the position of queen, the most important woman in the palace harem,

---

25. For a carefully written review of the conquests of Babylonia and Persia, see Yaakov Yosef Reinman, *Destiny*, pp. 120–138. On the Book of Esther in particular, Rabbi Nosson Scherman, "An Overview—The Period of the Miracle," The Book of Esther, pp. xv–xxxviii. "*Megillah*," *Mo'ed* 4, p. 68. On Vashti: "*Megillah*," *Mo'ed* 4, pp. 58–59; 70–71, 117. On the Banquest of Ahasuerus: "*Megillah*," *Mo'ed* 4, pp.70–73.

26. "*Megillah*," pp. 75–79. On the significance of silence, M. Sofer, "The Power of Silence," *Yated Ne'eman* (July 9, 1999), p. 64.

Esther remained silent and patient. How so? Mordecai had advised his wife to withhold any information about herself, her past, or her wishes; she was not to speak about anything personal. Mordecai and Esther knew that there had to be a divine reason for her place in the palace. But neither had any idea of what that reason was, though it must have been important and crucial. Thus Esther had to be patient and silent, and so she was for all twelve years—until now. Unlike Esther, Mordecai was known to be Jewish. In addition, he took very daring steps such as refusing to bow down to Persians, the enemies of the Jewish people. This constituted a risk to all the Jewish people and was an immediate cause for Haman's eagerness to have the king of Persia give his approval to have all the Jews wiped out one day in the following year, the day we now know as Purim.[27]

When this news began to spread, Mordecai again took drastic action. He wore sackcloth and ashes, shouting in the streets that the Jews were to be obliterated on the fourteenth of the Jewish month of Adar.[28]

What was Esther doing now? She sent a note to Mordecai and a suit of clothes to replace the sackcloth and ashes; in short she wished him to behave in a more civilized way and find other means to save the Jews. Her ways would be womanly, indirect rather than confrontational. All the years until now she had never made a single move to approach the king, to be made attractive for him, or to say anything about herself. Instead, hiding her inner radiance and glory, she would listen, and listen, and listen.[29]

ESTHER AWAITS A SIGN FROM GOD

And now Esther was awaiting a sign from above, a sign that God was to favor the Jews. Realizing that Esther was taking no action, Mordecai sent her a cogent and powerful message:

27. "*Megillah,*" p.117.

28. *The Book of Esther,* 4:1–3.

29. *The Book of Esther,* As a passive object of Ahasuerus' embraces, Esther is not seen as an active partner: "*Sanhedrin,*" *Nezikin,* trans. H. Freedman (London: the Soncino Press, 1935), p. 504.

Do not imagine that you will be able to escape in the king's palace any more than the rest of the Jews. For if you persist in keeping silent at a time like this, relief and deliverance will come to the Jews from some other place, while you and your father's house will perish. And who knows whether it was just for such a time as this that you attained the royal position![30]

In reply, Esther asked that all the Jews in Shushan be assembled to fast for three days and nights for her sake. Esther and her maidens would fast as well. She promised "Then I will go in to the king though it's unlawful. And if I perish, I perish."[31] Mordecai did everything that Esther instructed him to do. Still Esther proceeded to behave in a manner not at all confrontational. Using her powers of female understanding and sensitivity, she risked her life by standing in the courtyard facing the throne of the king, although he had not summoned her to come. Her silent and restrained behavior all those troublesome years had prepared her way for this moment. Three angels had also been appointed to help her. Thus the king extended his scepter to her and, instead of ordering that she be killed for such effrontery, he said, "What is your petition, Queen Esther? Even if it be half the kingdom, it shall be given you."[32]

QUEEN ESTHER USES HER CUNNING

One would have expected Esther to begin her persuasive plea at once. Surely other great women in the Bible have done so: Rachel to Hashem, little Miriam to her father, Hannah to Eli, the priest, and Abigail to King David. But those women were approaching men who were good men, people of God who simply lacked the clarity that the women had at that moment. This time, knowing that she faced a dangerous adversary, Queen Esther had to use her cunning.

---

30. *The Book of Esther*, 4:13–14.

31. *The Book of Esther*, "*Megillah*," p. 88.

32. *The Book of Esther*, 5.3. "The holy spirit clothed her," "*Megillah*," pp. 85, 89, 91.

She simply invited the king and Haman to come to a feast that she would prepare for them.

At this feast, the king again asked Esther about her request but, strange to say, she repeated her invitation that they join her at a second feast the next day. That night the king, unable to sleep, passed the night reviewing notes in his great book. There he discovered a reference to Mordecai's discovery that saved his life. Just then, Haman appeared, bent on securing the king's approval of the destruction of the Jews because Mordecai had refused to bow down to Haman. Before Haman could open his mouth, the king asked what he would do for a person of whom the king approved. *Oh,* thought Haman, *the king must be referring to me.* Of course Haman then described an outstanding tribute: give him the king's horse and crown and, with the favored one seated on the horse, have someone lead him through the streets of Persia, announcing, "This is what is done for the man whom the king especially wants to honor." Imagine the chagrin of Haman when the king directed him to lead Mordecai throughout the city in this fashion (although he would not be wearing the crown of the king).[33]

Through the palace window, Esther watched, undoubtedly with great joy, for now she knew that God was favoring her people. Awaiting just such a clue, she could move forward to tell the king of Haman's plan to destroy her people. Brilliantly, she phrased the news in terms of the harm and danger that Haman would be bringing, not to her people alone, but most of all to the king himself! To destroy God's people when this had never been foretold would surely arouse the enmity of God. It is very likely that a loss of funds for the king's treasury was alluded to as well.[34]

Mordecai and Esther saved the Jewish people from total extinction. Esther requested that the rabbis put the story of Purim in a book. When they hesitated for fear of upsetting the gentile nations, Esther, the queen, reminded them that the nations already knew. And so it was done. Esther's brilliant plea to the king, rich with womanly understanding and insight, succeeded at once. The king saw to it that Haman and his family were executed. Ironically,

---

33. *The Book of Esther,* 6:6 ff. "*Megillah,*" pp. 94 ff.
34. *The Book of Esther,* 7:1 ff; "*Megillah,*" pp. 96 ff.

Haman was hung on the very scaffold built according to the specifications set by Haman for the destruction of Mordecai.[35]

SUBTLE AND POWERFUL ARE
THE WORDS OF WOMEN

The restraint of Esther and the words of Abigail and Huldah suggest how subtle and powerful are the words of women. The gift to women of nine of the ten powers of speech holds also a danger of words that may be inappropriate. Negatively, the words of Eve to Adam changed the face of the world and of all mankind. In contrast, Sarah's words to Abraham had to be listened to, for God told Abraham to "listen to the voice of Sarah." Abigail's words to David are eloquent, clear, and compelling. So much so that they stopped him literally in his tracks and cleared the path to his kingship. Huldah's prophecy provided the stimulus needed by King Josiah to abolish all pagan worship in Israel. In one way or another, the words of women are significant.

ONLY HUMANS HAVE POWER
OF SPEECH AND RESTRAINT

Only humankind has the power of speech and the built-in ability to restrain from speaking. Unlike other species who respond by reflex to a situation, human beings go through a process. A situation presents itself, we think about it, and if it seems crucial, we take immediate action, by deciding to speak, store the information, or respond at another time. We make decisions because we are thinking creatures. When the decision needs action, we choose whether to respond or not. The choice is ours. In order to make the best choice, we must listen to our inner voice, wherein lies our deepest connection with God. It is He Who is showing the way. To speak out or to remain silent are choices with which He has blessed us, but often difficult choices to make.

---

35. "When did all the ends of the earth see the salvation of the Lord? In the day of Mordecai and Esther," "*Megillah,*" p. 60. Esther sent to the wise men requesting a book and a festival, "*Megillah,*" pp. 34–35.

Edna had been married for twelve years to Oscar. A businessman, he had been successful and generous to both his wife and son,
Adam. A homemaker by choice, Edna enjoyed her role, especially
that of wife and mother. They appreciated Adam, now 8 years old,
for being a sweet, bright, and cooperative child. The trio was bonded
and doing well. Oscar revealed little about his work to Edna but instead, and to her delight, seemed very interested in her daily life. Many
of her women friends told her that this was a rarity among men, complaining that men only wanted to talk about their business, and payed
little attention to the routines of their wives. Edna felt privileged. And
then the bubble broke. Oscar, a man of patience and calm, changed.
Jumpy, nervous, he snapped at her. When at first she asked what
was wrong, he said, "Nothing. Something is happening at work. It
will pass." But Oscar became more and more irritable and, one day,
when he slapped Adam for the first time, she demanded to know what
was going on. Hesitating and groping for words, he told her that he
had been called before the Security Exchange Commission. He was
under investigation and did not know what would happen. Edna was
in shock. A million questions raced through her mind: How could
she not have known what was happening? Would he go to jail? What
could she say to people and most critically, what could she tell their
son, Adam, who adored his father?

EDNA DECIDES TO DO THE SENSIBLE THING

She decided to do the sensible thing. She would stand by her husband in his moment of need and try to get to the root of the legal
implications and his responsibilities as a businessman. She would
refrain from telling Adam anything detrimental about his father. She
obtained information about the SEC and its workings. She became
aware that Oscar had used information that he was not authorized
to reveal in order to buy stocks and make money. While hugely disappointed in the man she had trusted as a person of integrity, she
knew she would stand by him. The pressing issue was how to handle
Adam without destroying his adoring image of his father and at the
same time, help him recognize that his parent, like all humans, has
flaws.

For the year before the trial was to take place, Edna told Adam
that his daddy would seem nervous at times because he was hav-

ing difficulty in the business. She explained that they needed to be patient and try to help him. Adam could help by being sensitive. When he perceived his father was having a difficult time, he was not to take it as personal rejection. Instead, he could ask when it would be a good time to talk to him. Adam did so. Edna would not reveal the possibility of jail to her son until it was an actuality. This took much holding back. Seared with pain, she often wanted to shout, "Why is this happening to me? How can I handle it all? How could I have not seen this? Was any of this my fault? What will become of our family? What will people say? How will my son be affected once all of this is known?" Yet she was able to deal with her agony without pouring any of it on her child. She knew in her mother's heart that this would be hurtful to the son she loved.

More than a year after Oscar had revealed his dilemma to her, the trial took place. He was sentenced to two to five years in Federal prison. Edna poured her heart out to her mother and her rabbi. Both offered solace and support. She did not ask them what to tell Adam. She needed to feel it in her heart and act out of her own consciousness, along with her deep understanding of her son. She broke the news to Adam. Her basic message was "Daddy did something wrong. He had a secret and didn't keep it. He has to go to jail. We will write to him and visit him if we can, but you will be with me and know that Daddy loves you even when he is away from you."

Life went on. When Oscar had been away for a while, and Edna and Adam had shared more and more time together, she explained to him that based upon their tradition, everything has a purpose. No matter how terrible a thing seems at the time it is happening, there is always some divine plan at play and as Jews, we must trust it. She emphasized that every opportunity, even being in jail, can be used for the good. Daddy had told her that he had more time for reading, something he always loved and had had little time for. He was getting to know some inmates with whom he could have intense discussions about matters that were interesting to him. He was also using this time productively as an extended period for reflection. He had done something wrong. He knew now that he had to change his life. This was the message to him, and he planned to act on it. None of this had happened by chance, he said. And most importantly, it would never happen again. This he promised his wife and son.

Edna used caution in telling others about her family's situation. Each word was carefully considered. At no time did she besmirch her husband's name. She continued to see her rabbi for advice. She felt strong and comfortable within herself, and closer than ever to her son. Time alone for the two of them made for further bonding. Both wrote to Oscar, and Edna visited as often as possible, telling Adam all the details of the visit that he would be interested in. When Oscar was depressed and sad, she withheld that from Adam, knowing that at his age it would not be helpful knowledge.

OSCAR IS RELEASED FROM PRISON

After several years, Oscar was released from prison. Since Edna had been selective in the information she disclosed to the community, family and friends welcomed him warmly. Their response was simply, "Let's give him a chance. Who are we to judge? Only God can judge and He does so with mercy." Life returned to the family. No longer under court rulings, Oscar returned to work. He had, he said, "learned his lesson." Over and over again, he told his wife how hugely appreciative he was of her love, care, and support. He was especially thankful that although she must have felt much pain and despair, never once did she "run loose at the mouth." Like Esther, she was able to monitor herself. She used a careful blending of heart and mind to make decisions that would benefit not only herself but also those she loved most. Like many women in today's world, she did it magnificently.

Daily life may pulse with drama. Edna had to hand-feed information to her son so as not to contaminate his development as a loving person. But at times silence is the best resource. Total silence, a withdrawing of our splendid ability to use words, is difficult for us all. Yet it can be done.

MONA WAS A YOUNG WIDOW

Mona was a young widow. At thirty-seven, her beloved husband had passed away. She mourned him and devoted herself to her two children: Lenore, aged 12 and Noah, aged 10. Remarrying never entered her mind. But unexpected events do take place. A friend told Mona that she was inviting a few people over whom she felt Mona would like to meet. There she met Barry, a man who had recently lost his wife. Both Barry and Mona were interested in each other and after a year of courtship they decided to marry. Never having had children, due to his wife's long-term illness, Barry instantly became a devoted father. Noah was grateful and responded to him with enthusiasm. Lenore, quite the opposite, was vehement in her lack of responsiveness. Whenever Barry made any suggestions to her or offered to help, she told him, "You're not my father. I don't have to take any orders from you." Mona cringed when she heard her daughter talk this way but decided not to intervene. She knew in her heart that eventually the two would work things out. Her interference would split the family. She did not want to take sides and alienate her daughter or her husband. It was difficult. At times her impulse was to jump in, particularly when Lenore was rude to the man who was doing his best to be a parent to her. But she remained silent. Before parents' day Lenore said to her mother, "Next Tuesday is parents' day and Mrs. Levinson would like to talk to you. She's a good teacher, Mom. I hope you get to see her." When Mona told her that both she and Barry would be available, her reply was as predicted: "Don't you get it, Mom? Barry is *your* husband. He is *not* my father and it is parents' day *not* mother's new-husband's day." Mona held her tongue. But Barry did accompany her to meet and talk to Lenore's teacher. Barry told this to Lenore who sulked but said nothing.

Barry had a younger sister, Nancy, with whom he was very close. During his wife's terminal illness, Nancy had been devoted to him, acting as his confidante. She was one to whom he could reveal his heart; he could count on her to be there for him. Nancy was married and had a young daughter of four, Danielle. She was a bright, outgoing, and pretty child, simply a joy to be with. Living close by, Nancy and Danielle visited Barry and Mona once a week. When Danielle saw Lenore brushing her hair into a ponytail, she asked, "Lenore, could you brush my hair and put in a pretty ribbon like you have?" Lenore's answer was brusque and to the point. "No. I can't. Let your mother do that." And she would walk away. Mona, disappointed said nothing.

MONA'S RESTRAINT UNIFIES THE FAMILY

Lenore was having difficulty in school. Math was not her strong point and she was falling behind. One day, Lenore was moaning over the fact that she was not prepared for the coming exam: "This math, I can't stand it. I just don't get it." Barry, who taught math at the local high school, intervened. "Lenore, let me help you. I can show you some shortcuts that will help. I've shown them to some of my poorest math students, and they became some of the best. I know you can, too. You're so smart. It will only take a few minutes." Reluctantly, Lenore consented. "OK," she said. "Anything to get out of this yucky mess."

Exam time came and Lenore, while not at the top of the class, received a grade far beyond her expectations. Mrs. Levinson handed her the exam and said, "Lenore, I'm so glad you did well. Frankly, I was surprised. I am delighted. How did it happen?" Lenore's response was, as she told Mona and Barry, "It was a miracle."

A short time later, Nancy and Danielle came to visit. This time Lenore approached the little niece. "Honey," she said, "would you like me to put up your hair? I bought a new pink ribbon that will look great in your dark hair. I'll do it for you if you want me to." Danielle looked ecstatic. Jumping up and down, she shouted, "Yeah, yeah. Lenore is going to brush my hair and give me her new ribbon." She ran to hug Lenore. Lenore kissed her and, taking her gently by the hand, with a hairbrush and shiny, new ribbon dangling from her fingers, walked her into her room and closed the door. When they came out a short time later—Danielle in her new hairdo—everyone clapped. Barry, beaming, thanked Lenore. Her answer, was, "No problem." After a moment, she added, "You deserve it, Barry. I may never be a math genius, but at least I'll get through."

The family was once more a family. Unlikely though it may seem, remaining silent is at times the road to take.

Recommended Resources

Biblical Women in the Midrash: A Sourcebook
By Naomi M. Hyman   0-7657-6030-4

**A Book of Jewish Women's Prayers: Translations
from the Yiddish**
Selected, compiled, translated, and edited by Norman Tarnor
                                                     1-56821-298-4

The Book of Jewish Women's Tales
Retold by Barbara Rush   0-7657-5981-0

**Letters to My Daughter: A Father Writes
about Torah and the Jewish Woman**
By Walter Orenstein   1-56821-387-5

**Out of the Depths I Call to You: A Book of Prayers
for the Married Jewish Woman**
Edited and translated by Nina Beth Cardin   1-56821-411-1

**Which Lilith?" Feminist Writers Re-Create
the World's First Woman**
Edited by Enid Dame, Lilly Rivlin, and Henny Wenkart
                                                     0-7657-6015-0

The Woman in Jewish Law and Tradition
By Michael Kaufman   1-56821-624-6

The Women of the Talmud
By Judith Z. Abrams   1-56821-283-6

The Women of the Torah: Commentaries from the Talmud, Midrash, and Kabbalah
By Barbara L. Thaw Ronson   0-7657-9991-X

The Woman of Valor: *Eshet Hayil*
Commentary by Adin Steinsaltz
Illustrated by Itzhak Tordjman   1-56821-378-6

Available at
your local bookstore,
online at www.aronson.com,
or by calling toll-free 1-800-782-0015

Index

About the Authors

Dr. Blema Feinstein received her doctorate from The City University of New York. She is the author of numerous articles in Jewish publications including *Bas Ayin, Amit Women,* and *Midstream.* Dr. Feinstein is a well-known lecturer and workshop leader in the U.S. and Canada, teaching groups connected with The Jewish Heritage Center, Ohr Somayach, Sisterhoods, Seed Summer Learning Institute, various Y's, Amit Women, Hadassah, Brandeis University Women, Chabad Centers, and others. Dr. Feinstein resides in Long Island; recently widowed, she has two daughters, Golda and Emily.

Dr. Marcella Bakur Weiner received her doctorate from Columbia University and her post-doctorate certificate in psychoanalytic training from the Mental Health Institute in New York City. A former Senior Research Scientist for the New York State Department of Mental Hygiene, she has been on faculty at Columbia University, City and Brooklyn Colleges of the C.U.N.Y., and Fordham University. Dr. Weiner is the author or co-author of numerous books and articles. Currently a Fellow of the American Psychological Association (APA), Dr. Weiner is also President of the Advisory Council of the Mapleton-Midwood Mental Health Center in Brooklyn, NY and on faculty at Marymount Manhattan College in New York City. Dr. Weiner is the mother of two adult sons, Lawrence and Steven, and resides with her husband, Will, in Brooklyn, New York. She maintains a private practice in Brooklyn and Manhattan.